# VOLUME 5

# VIETNAM · JAPAN · THAILAND KOREA · MALAYSIA · INDONESIA

D1133516

LES ÉDITIONS
TRANScript
PUBLISHING

ISBN 2-921488-43-4

# Southeast Asia: INDOCHINA

S imple, exquisitely flavoured soup, fish, meat and poultry dishes are highlights of Laos, Cambodia and Vietnam, three countries of Indochina. Ginger beef soup, mackerel with fresh tomato sauce, and fried chicken with lemon grass are just some of the local favourites.

Indochina is bordered by Thailand, the Gulf of Thailand and the South China Sea. The Mekong River, one of the world's greatest, forms a natural border between Laos and Thailand and runs through Cambodia and Vietnam before it empties into the South China Sea. This gives the region an

*A lakeside stilt village in Cambodia*

3

abundance of both sea and river fish, most of them types unknown in the West. There are good Western substitutes, however, so that the flavourful fish dishes of Indochina can be made by adventurous cooks.

Both Chinese and French influences are apparent in the cookery, but the individual cuisines are still paramount. The French introduced the temperate fruits and vegetables of Europe into the region which resulted in a great abundance of fruits and vegetables of both tropical and temperate zones. Though the region lies in the tropics, temperate produce grows well in the highland, giving the best of both worlds from the cook's point of view. Many of the inhabitants are Buddhist, so there are lots of vegetarian dishes and many dishes using only small amounts of meat and fish.

Unlike our meals, which are highly structured with courses following one another, the food in an Indochinese meal comes to the table all at the same time. There is a soup, two main dishes of different types and usually an undressed leafy salad highly flavoured with fresh herbs. This is rice-eating territory and each diner receives a large bowl of rice which is refilled as often as needed.

All food is served in bowls and there are always bowls of sauce available for dipping. It is usually a sauce known as fish gravy, fish sauce or fish soy. It is essential in Southeast Asian cookery and called *nuoc nam* in Vietnam and *nam pla* in Thailand. Made from fresh anchovies layered with salt and allowed to ferment in barrels, it flavours and salts food at the same time. The smell may seem disagreeable to the unfamiliar nose at first sniff but when used in cooking, or as a dipping sauce, the flavour is entirely delicious.

Coriander leaves are also used a great deal in the three cuisines, as are bean curd (tofu), noodles, coconut, fresh chilies, garlic,

spring onions and shallots. Lemon grass is also often used. It is hard to find this fresh plant, with its spring onion-like bulb, because lemon grass needs a tropical or semi-tropical or climate to flourish. Fortunately, lemon grass can be bought dried or ground.

The lettuce used is soft round lettuce and the cabbage is our Chinese cabbage, often known as Chinese leaves. Red chilies are preferred in Indochina but green ones will do as well. Freshly ground black pepper is used often, and to a lesser extent, white pepper. Long-grain rice is the rice of everyday eating in Vietnam and Cambodia. In Laos, short-grain glutinous rice is more widely eaten, though it is very popular in all three countries.

## Unusual ingredients

Thai fish sauce or fish gravy, *nam pla* in Thai, *nuoc nam* in Vietnamese, is a thin, light brown liquid made from fermented, salted anchovies. An essential flavouring in many Indochinese dishes, it is sold at Chinese food stores.

**Glutinous rice**, also known as "sweet" or "sticky" rice, is a short-grained rice that is widely eaten, mainly in Southeast Asia. Glutinous rice needs a different cooking method from that used for long-grained rice. After washing it is boiled hard for 1 minute, then drained, covered and cooked on an asbestos mat over a very low heat for 15-20 minutes.

**Ground lemon grass**, also known as *sereh* powder, is available at many Indian shops and Oriental markets. It has a strong taste and a smell of lemon and should be used sparingly. Use grated lemon zest as a substitute.

***Laos* or galingale** is a commonly used spice in the East. It is a tuber that looks like ginger root. *Laos* is usually sold ground at Oriental food stores. Ginger can be used instead although the flavor is quite different. ■

# ■ LAOTIAN CHICKEN SALAD

- *20 minutes*
- *Serves 2-4*

**30 mL (2 tbls) vegetable oil**
**275 g (10 oz) bean curd (tofu)**
**225 g (8 oz) cooked chicken breast**
  **or thigh, boned and shredded**
**2 large fresh hot red or green**
  **chilies or 2-4 mL (1/2 - 3/4 tsp)**
  **red hot pepper flakes**
**1 cucumber**
**2 tomatoes**
**175 mL (3/4 cup) fresh mint leaves,**
  **coarsely chopped**
**45 mL (3 tbls) roasted peanuts,**
  **ground**
**2 green onions chopped**
**30 mL (2 tbls) Thai fish sauce**
**30 mL (2 tbls) lemon or lime juice**
**50 mL (2 fl oz) thick coconut milk**
**10 mL (2 tsp) sugar**
**8 sprigs of coriander leaves or**
  **parsley, to garnish**

● Heat the oil in a small frying-pan and sauté the bean curd until it is lightly browned on both sides, 1-2 minutes. Lift it out onto a board or plate with a spatula, allow it to cool; cut into 15 mm (1/2 in) cubes.

● Transfer the bean curd cubes to a salad bowl. Add the chicken. Halve the chilies across, remove the seeds, then cut into fine lengthways strips and add them to the bowl.

● Peel the cucumber, halve it lengthways, scrape out the seeds with a teaspoon, then cut it into thin slices and add them to the bowl. Dip the tomatoes into boiling water for 30 seconds, skin and halve them and squeeze out the seeds. Slice the flesh and add it to the salad bowl.

● Mix together the mint leaves, peanuts, spring onion, fish sauce, lemon juice, coconut milk and sugar in a small bowl. Pour the dressing over the salad ingredients and lightly toss. Garnish with the coriander sprigs and serve.

Use canned cocunut milk and follow the recipe for thick *santen* given in the section on Indonesia on page 60.

*Laotian chicken salad*

# ■ GINGER BEEF SOUP

- *3 hours 30 minutes*
- *Serves 8*

**700 g (1 1/2 lb) oxtail, cut into chunks**
**700 g (1 1/2 lb) stewing beef in one piece**
**1 garlic clove, chopped**
**6 green onions, stems and bulbs chopped separately or 2 onions, chopped**
**5 cm (2 in) piece fresh ginger root, peeled**
**1 star anise**
**green part of 6 green onions, chopped**
**60 mL (4 tbls) chopped fresh coriander leaves**
**1 large onion, halved, then very thinly sliced**

**250 mL (1 cup) bean sprouts**
**225 g (8 oz) beef fillet or sirloin in one slice**
**225 g (8 oz) rice stick noodles**
**30 mL (2 tbls) Thai fish sauce**
**5 mL (1 tsp) salt**
**pinch of monosodium glutamate**
**1 lime or lemon cut into 8 wedges**
**1-2 fresh hot red chilies, seeded and sliced or 2-5 mL (1/2-1 tsp) hot pepper flat**

● Put the oxtail, garlic, shallot bulbs, ginger root and star anise in a large saucepan with 2 L (9 cups) cold water. Bring the liquid to a boil over medium heat, skim, lower the heat and simmer, covered, for 1 hour. Add the stewing steak and continue to simmer over low heat until the meats are tender, about 2 hours.

*Ginger beef soup*

● ● ● ● ● ● ● ● ● ● ● ● ● ● ● ● ● ● ● ● ● ● ● ●

● Meanwhile, combine the chopped green onion stems with the coriander leaves in a small bowl. Put the sliced onion into another bowl. Drop the bean sprouts into boiling water for 30 seconds, drain, rinse in cold water and put them into another bowl. Put the tenderloin beef into the freezer to chill fo 30 minutes.

● Bring a large saucepan of water to a boil and add the rice stick noodles. Bring the water back to a boil over high heat and boil for 3 minutes. Drain the noodles in a colander, rinse in cold water, then drain thoroughly. Cut the chilled beef into the thinnest possible slices and reserve them in a bowl.

● Lift the cooked meats out of the soup and, when they are cool enough to handle, bone the oxtail and slice the chuck or stewing meat. Add the fish sauce, salt and monosodium glutamate to the soup. Return the meats to the soup and heat through.

● Have ready a large bowl for each guest. Divide the noodles between the bowls, top with the cooked meats, then add the thin slices of raw beef. Add about half of the onion slices, then some beans sprouts and a little of the mixed coriander and green onion stems. Have the hot soup ready and fill up each bowl; the heat from the soup will cook the raw beef.

● At the table, guests add more bean sprouts and onion and squeeze lime or lemon juice into the soup if wished. The chopped fresh chilies and extra fish gravy are served separately, to be added to taste.

# ■ CABBAGE and PORK SOUP

- *30 minutes*
- *Serves 4*

**1.25 L (5 cups) chicken stock**
**6 green onions, white and green parts, chopped**
**400 mL (1 5/8 cup) coriander leaves, chopped**
**1.25 L (5 cups) Chinese celery cabbage, chopped**
**15 mL (1 tbls) Thai fish sauce**
**6 shallots or 2 small onions, peeled and sliced**
**100 g (4 oz) minced lean pork**
**salt (optional)**
**2 medium-sized eggs**
**freshly ground black pepper**
**chopped coriander leaves, to garnish**

● Combine the stock, green onions and coriander in a saucepan. Cover and simmer over medium heat for 15 minutes, then strain and discard the solids.

● Bring the soup back to a simmer and add the Chinese cabbage, fish sauce, shallots and pork. Taste for seasoning, add salt if necessary, and simmer, covered, for 15 minutes.

● Break the eggs into the soup, stirring quickly with chopsticks or a fork so that the eggs form threads. Pour the soup into bowls, season with black pepper to taste, and garnish with coriander leaves.

# ■ VEGETABLE SALAD

*This is a typical Vietnamese salad assortment, though other vegetables may be added.*
*There is no dressing as the mint and coriander provide the perfect balance to the lettuce and*
*the cucumber.*

* *10 minutes*
* *Serves 6*

**1 soft round lettuce, washed and
    dried**
**1/2 cucumber**
**175 mL (3/4 cup) fresh mint leaves,
    stalks removed**
**175 mL (3/4 cup) fresh coriander
    leaves, stalks removed**
**meat, fish, shellfish or poultry dish,
    to serve**

● Make a mound of lettuce leaves in
the centre of a platter. Cut strips of
peel lengthways from the cucumber,
leaving alternate unpeeled strips. Cut the
cucumber in half lengthways and scrape
out the seeds with a spoon into thin slices.
Arrange the slices round the edge of the
platter.

● Make mounds of mint and coriander
leaves round the lettuce and serve as a
side salad with any Vietnamese meat,
fish, shellfish or poultry dish.

*Vegetable salad*

● ● ● ● ● ● ● ● ● ● ● ● ● ● ● ● ● ● ● ● ● ● ●

# ■ MACKEREL with TOMATO SAUCE

*This simple dish is typical of Vietnamese cooking. Fresh tomato, borrowed from the New World, makes a wonderful sauce when combined with traditional oriental fish gravy.*

- *20 minutes*
- *Serves 4*

**1 mackerel, cleaned, weighing about 450 g (1 lb) without head or tail**
**75 mL (1/3 cup) oil**
**2 garlic cloves, thinly sliced**
**the white part of 2 green onions, sliced**
**2-3 tomatoes, blanched, skinned and diced**
**30 mL (2 tbls) Thai fish sauce**
**15 mL ( 1 tbls) sugar**
**freshly ground black pepper**
**plain boiled rice, to serve**

● Pat the fish dry with absorbent paper. In a wok or a heavy frying-pan large enough to hold the fish comfortably, heat 60 mL (1/4 cup) of the oil over medium heat. Sauté the fish until it is browned on both sides and cooked through, about 5 minutes on each side, transfer to a serving dish and keep warm.
● Discard the oil in the wok or frying-pan and wipe it clean. Heat the rest of the oil and then add the garlic and green onions. Cook, stirring, over medium heat, until they are lightly browned, about 1 minute.
● Add the tomato, fish sauce, sugar and a generous amount of black pepper. Stir to mix, bring to a simmer and cook, stirring, for 2 minutes. Pour the sauce over the fish and serve immediately with rice.

● ● ● ● ● ● ● ● ● ● ● ● ● ● ● ● ● ● ● ● ● ● ● ● ●

# ■ CAULIFLOWER with PADDY-STRAW MUSHROOMS

- *Serves 4*

**1 small cauliflower cut into florets**
**the white part of a leek, cleaned, sliced and thoroughly washed**
**15 mL (1 tbls) soy sauce**
**2 mL (1/2 tsp) sugar**
**15 mL (1 tbls) oil**
**125 g (4 oz) canned paddy-straw mushrooms, drained**

● Slice the cauliflower lengthways into thin slices and reserve. Mix the soy sauce, 15 mL (1 tbls) water and sugar together in a small bowl.
● Heat the oil in a wok or a frying-pan over medium-low heat and sauté the leek for 1 minute. Add the cauliflower and cook, stirring, for 1 minute. Pour in 15-30 mL (1-2 tbls) cold water, cover and simmer over low heat for 2-3 minutes.
● Add the paddy-straw mushrooms and the soy sauce mixture and continue to cook, covered, for 2-3 minutes. Serve at once.

● ● ● ● ● ● ● ● ● ● ● ● ● ● ● ● ● ● ● ● ● ● ● ● ●

# ■ BEEF with CELERY and GREEN PEPPER

- *30 minutes chilling, plus 20 minutes*
- *Serves 4*

**225 g (8 oz) top rump beef, chilled for 30 minutes then very thinly sliced**
**20 mL (4 tsp) Thai fish sauce**
**freshly ground black pepper**
**15 mL (1 tbls) cornstarch**
**5 mL (1 tsp) white wine vinegar**
**5 mL (1 tsp) sugar**
**15 mL (1 tbls) vegetable oil**
**1 large garlic clove, chopped**
**1 green pepper, seeded and cut into 5 mm (1/4 in) strips**

**4 celery stalks with leaves, cut diagonally into 5 mm (1/4 in) slices**
**2 tomatoes, each cut into 4 wedges**
**1 onion, cut into 4 wedges**
**glutinous rice, to serve**

● Put the sliced beef into a bowl and pour 15 mL (3 tsp) of the fish sauce over it. Sprinkle generously with pepper, mix well and marinate for 15 minutes.

● In another bowl combine the cornstarch, remaining fish sauce, 125 mL (1/2 cup) water, vinegar and sugar, and set aside.

● Heat the oil over fairly high heat in a frying-pan or wok. Add the garlic and beef and stir-fry with chopsticks (preferably) or a fork for 1 minute. Add the green pepper, celery, tomatoes and onion and cook 1 minute, stirring. Add the cornstarch mixture and cook, stirring, for 2 minutes longer. Serve immediately with rice.

You can use sliced meat such as the frozen beef slices sold for Chinese fondue.

*Serve a red Californian Cabernet Sauvignon, tannic and woodsy with this single dish.*

# ■ FISH in COCONUT MILK

*Catfish, a great favourite, would be used in Indochina for this recipe. However, a firm flesh fish can also be used, such as seabass, halibut, tuna or sword-fish.*

- *20 minutes soaking,*
  *plus about 30 minutes*
- *Serves 4*

**3-4 large dried red chilies, seeded and shredded**
**or 2-5 mL (1/2-1 tsp) hot red pepper flakes**
**225 mL (8 fl oz) thick coconut milk**
**450 mL (12 fl oz) thin coconut milk**
**10 garlic cloves, chopped**
**5 cm (2 in) slice of lime or large strip lemon zest**
**5 mL (1 tsp) ground ginger**
**15 mL (1 tbls) ground lemon grass**
**450 g (1 lb) fish cut into 4 equal serving pieces**
**15 mL (1 tbls) Thai fish sauce**
**30 mL (2 tbls) roasted peanuts, chopped**
**fresh basil leaves or sprigs of coriander leaves, to garnish**
**2-3 fresh hot green chilies, seeded and cut into strips (optional)**
**boiled rice, to serve**

● Soak the dried chilies in a small bowl in warm water to cover until they are soft, about 20 minutes.

● Drain, then grind the chilies to a paste in a mortar or small blender with the garlic, lime or lemon zest, ground ginger and lemon grass, using some chili water.

● In a wok or a frying-pan, heat the thick coconut milk over low heat and cook until it becomes oily, stirring from time to time. Add the garlic and chili paste and cook, stirring, for 1-2 minutes. Add the fish and the fish sauce and cook for five minutes.

● Add the thin coconut milk and simmer gently until the fish is done, about 10 minutes. Stir in the chopped peanuts. Transfer the fish to a heated serving plate, using a fish slice. Pour the sauce over, garnish with fresh basil or coriander sprigs and the chili strips, if wished. Serve the dish with rice.

> *Use canned coconut milk*
> *or prepare the recipes for thin and*
> *thick santen given in the section*
> *on Indonesia on page 60.*

# ■ CAMBODIAN FRUIT SALAD

*This simple and refreshing fruit salad gets its unusual taste from lichees.*

- *35 minutes, plus 2-3 hours chilling*
- *Serves 4*

**1 medium-sized grapefruit, peeled and sectioned**
**1 medium-sized orange, peeled and sectioned**
**1 small pineapple, peeled, cored and cubed, or 1 can (796 mL/28 oz) pineapple cubes**
**14 fresh lichees, peeled, seeded and cut in two or 1 can (796 mL/28 oz) lichees, drained and halved, reserving juice**
**15 mL (1 tbls) sugar (optional)**
**5 mL (1 tsp) lemon or lime juice**

● Remove any seeds and white pith from the grapefruit and orange sections and cut them across into halves.

● In a glass dessert bowl combine the orange and grapefruit sections with the pineapple and lichees. Add 30 mL (2 tbls) of the reserved lichee syrup (if using canned fruit), or sprinkle with the sugar. Add the lemon or lime juice and mix lightly. Chill for at least 2 hours before serving.

*Cambodian fruit salad*

• • • • • • • • • • • • • • • • • • • • • • • •

# JAPAN

Japan, isolated for hundreds of years, has a quite different cuisine from the rest of the Orient. It is most famous for its exquisitely arranged raw fish and seaweed dishes, but also has beautiful, tender beef and grows almost every variety of vegetable known in the West. Fruit is abundant too, especially the golden persimmon, called the "apple of the Orient."

Japanese food is elegantly simple. It is characterized by a natural taste and a strong feeling for using foods in their season; this feeling for seasonal cooking is called *kisetsukan*. There are summer noodle dishes, for instance, that are wonderfully cooling in summer's wilting heat but which chill to the bone in winter.

The Japanese are also very artistic in the kitchen. If a Japanese cook wishes to grate the large white radish, called *daikon*, with a dried red chili, he will poke a hole with chopsticks in the centre of the radish and put in the chili; the two are then grated together. The red and white is very pretty together and the Japanese call it "autumn leaves turning colour." There is also humour in the naming of dishes: a rice dish with chicken and eggs is called "parents and children" while another rice dish with beef and eggs translates as "strangers and children."

Until comparatively recently, food was cooked over charcoal and techniques, different from our usual chopping and slicing, were developed to cut ingredients thinly. The food then cooks quickly as a greater surface is exposed to the heat. Since all food is eaten with wooden chopsticks, it is cut into bite-sized pieces which are pretty to look at.

The Japanese meal structure is different from the Western pattern, the food being classified not by its place in the meal but by the cooking method. For example, *yakimono* are grilled foods, *gohan* are rice dishes and *mushi-*

*Preparing food in a Tokyo restaurant*

*mono* are steamed foods while *sashimi*, sliced raw fish, is not cooked at all. Seaweeds play an important role in Japanese cooking and the principal stock, *ichiban dashi*, usually shortened to dashi for convenience, is made from the seaweed *kombu* (a type of dried kelp found in natural food stores or oriental grocery stores) and finely flaked dried bonito fish. Packed versions of *dashi* are very good, as are almost all the packaged Japanese kitchen shortcuts. The soy bean in its various forms is also important such as the soy sauce, *shōyu*, bean curd, *nomen tōfu*, and red and white bean paste, *miso*. Many one-pot dishes, such as *sukiyaki*, are cooked at the table and served with rice and may provide a whole meal. *Sukiyaki* is probably the best-known Japanese dish. All the ingredients are brought to the table arranged decoratively on a serving platter and then cooked in a boiling pot of liquid by each person.

For a main meal there is always rice, a soup, a vegetable salad or a pickle dish, a fish or a shellfish, and a meat or poultry dish, all served in small portions. The food is presented all at once and not eaten in any particular order. The diners traditionally sit on cushions around a low table.

*Sake*, Japanese rice wine, is served warm in tiny sake cups, and may accompany the appetizers or be served throughout a festive meal. Wine is becoming increasingly popular, and dry white wine is probably the best choice. There is also excellent beer in Japan, and lovely, delicate green unfermented tea is served plain in tiny bowls.

### Unusual ingredients

**Daikon** is a very large, mild white radish. It is available in markets and vegetables shops as *mooli* and from Japanese food shops but young turnips can be substituted.

**Japanese rice vinegar** is a clear, light vinegar. As a subtitute, use cider or white wine vinegar in smaller quantities.

**Katsuobushi** is finely flaked, dried bonito fish. It can be bought at Japanese food shops, there is no substitute.

**Kombu** is dried kelp or seaweed. Buy it at Japanese food shops or health food shops.

**Mirin** is a sweet sake used only for cooking. There is no substitute. It is not expensive and can be bought at Japanese food shops.

**Miso** is a pungent, salty paste made from fermented soy beans. It can be red or white, the white being slightly sweeter. Monosodium glutamate (MSG) is the white salt of glutamic acid. It has no flavour of its own but brings out the flavour of other foods.

**Nori** is laver seaweed which is dried in flat sheets. It softens quickly when exposed to the air so toast lightly before using.

**Sake** is japanese rice wine. It is used in many dishes. Dry sherry is a less good substitute.

**Sansho** is Japanese pepper. It is sold ground at Japanese food shops. In Japan they often use the pepper leaf as a garnish.

**Shōyu** is Japanese soy sauce and is slightly different from Chinese soy sauce, being rather saltier and heavier. Kikkoman is a Japanese variety available in many supermarkets. Chinese soy sauce may be used.

**Shiritaki** are thin translucent Japanese noodles from the flour of a tuber. They are sold canned in water or in plastic bags.

**Sudare** is a square bamboo mat used for rolling up and squeezeing excess moisture out of soaked foods. A bamboo tablemat will do or use a clean kitchen cloth.

**Tofu** is a soft bean curd made from soy beans. It is sold in cubes in Chinese and Japanese food shops and can also be bought vacuum packed. Leftover tofu should be stored in an airtight container filled with water. Replace the water daily and keep refrigerated. The two varieties most often used are nomen tōfu (bean curd) and kinugoshi tofu (silky bean curd).

**Wasabi** is green horseradish powder. There is no substitute. ■

# ■ OMELETTE STUFFED with SPINACH

- 25 minutes
- Serves 4

**275 g (10 oz) fresh spinach,
   stalks removed
5 mL (1 tsp) sugar
10 mL (2 tsp) Japanese soy
   sauce (*shōyu*)
2-3 dashes monosodium glutamate
2 eggs
1 mL (1/4 tsp) salt
vegetable oil for frying**

● Wash the spinach thoroughly and drain. Put 2 L (9 cups) water into a large saucepan, and bring to a brisk oil. Drop in the spinach, add the sugar and boil over high heat for 2 minutes. Remove from heat and rinse the spinach 3 times in cold water, then squeeze out the moisture using a *sudare* or bamboo mat, or by hand.

● Sprinkle the spinach with the soy sauce and monosodium glutamate and form it into a roll. Divide it into 2 pieces and set aside.

● Break the eggs into a bowl, add the salt and stir with chopsticks until thoroughly blended but not foamy. Heat an omelette pan, or a 20 cm (8 in) frying-pan, and add just enough oil to coat the surface.

● Divide the eggs into 2 equal portions. Pour one portion into the omelette pan and tilt quickly so the egg covers the whole surface. When the egg is set and lightly browned on the underside, slide it out onto a bamboo mat or a cloth.

● Put one of the spinach rolls along the edge of the omelette and roll up the spinach in the omelette. Squeeze lightly to firm up the omelette roll.

● Repeat this procedure with the remaining egg and spinach and then leave the rolls to cool.

● When cold, cut the omelette into 2.5 cm (1 in) slices. Serve at room temperature.

*Omelette stuffed with spinach*

15

# ■ GRILLED MACKEREL FILLETS

- *15 minutes*
- *Serves 4*

**2 medium-sized mackerel fillets,
   with the skin**
**salt**
**250 mL (1 cup) *mooli* (*daikon*),
   grated**
**10 mL (2 tsp) soy sauce**

● Heat the grill. Cut the fillets in half crossways and sprinkle both sides with salt. Leave for 3 minutes.

● Rinse in cold water and pat dry with absorbent paper. Cut a shallow cross in the skin of each piece taking care not to cut through into the fish.

● Grill the fish about 7.5 cm (3 in) from the heat, for about 5 minutes on each side, turning once, until lightly browned on both sides.

● Arrange the fish on 4 medium-sized plates, skin side up. Lightly squeeze out the moisture from the grated radish. Form into mounds, one on each plate. Eat with chopsticks, putting a little radish on each small portion.

> *A refreshing cold beer
> will suffice with this no-fuss dish.
> Try a japanese one.*

# ■ JAPANESE STOCK (*DASHI*)

- *10 minutes*
- *Makes 1 L (4 1/2 cups)*

**10 cm (4 in) square piece dried kelp
   (*kombu*)**
**15 g (1/2 oz) flaked dried bonito
   (*katsuobushi*)**

● Rinse the kelp and cut a 1.5 cm (1/2 in) fringe along all four sides of the square.

● Pour 1.25 L (5 cups) water into a medium-sized saucepan. Add the seaweed and bring the water almost to the boil over a medium heat. Lift out the seaweed and reserve (see below).

● Bring the water to the boil and stir in the dried bonito flakes.

● Remove pan from the heat and stand for 2-3 minutes. Strain the liquid through a double thickness of damp muslin inside a sieve. The stock is now ready to be used. It will keep refrigerated for 2-3 days.

In Japan, the kelp and bonito flakes would be used to make a second stock for bean paste soups or for cooking vegetables. The second stock is made in exactly the same way, but with 700 mL (3 cups) water.

# ■ EGG DROP SOUP

- *10 minutes*
- *Serves 4*

**600 mL (2 1/2 cups) Japanese stock (*dashi* — see recipe, p. 60) or chicken broth**
**4 mL (3/4 tsp) salt**
**2.5 mL (1/2 tsp) Japanese soy sauce (*shöyu*)**
**15 mL (1 tbls) cornstarch, mixed with 30 mL (2 tbls) cold water**
**1 large egg, beaten and stirred with 15 mL (1 tbls) *dashi***
**5 mL (1 tsp) juice squeezed from grated fresh ginger root**

**■ TO GARNISH**
**lime or lemon peel (optional)**
**10 cm (4 in) square *nori* (optional)**

● Pour the stock into a medium-sized saucepan and bring it to the boil, covered. Season with salt and soy sauce and stir in the cornstarch mixture over a medium heat. Continue stirring until the soup is lightly thickened and smooth.

● Lower the heat so that the soup is barely simmering. Pour in the egg mixture through a flat skimmer or a sieve moving it in a circle over the soup. Cook for a few seconds longer to set the egg threads. Remove from the heat.

● Add the ginger juice. Pour the soup into bowls and garnish with pieces of lime or lemon peel cut into tiny V-shapes. If using, toast the seaweed on both sides for a few seconds and then crumble it over the soup.

*Egg drop soup*

# ■ RICE PATTIES TOPPED with RAW FISH

- *1 hour*
- *1 hour 30 minutes*
- *Serves 4 as a main course*

■ FOR THE PATTIES

**400 g (14 oz) short-grain rice**
**7.5 cm (3 in) square kelp (*kombu*),
cut into a 1.5 cm (1/2 in) fringe**
**60 mL (1/4 cup) Japanese rice
vinegar**
**15 mL (1 tbls) sugar**
**10 mL (2 tsp) salt**
**2.5 mL (1/2 tsp) monosodium
glutamate**

■ FOR THE TOPPING

**4 large raw large shrimps**
**4 fresh scallops**
**125 g (4 oz) salmon roes or 60 mL
(4 tbls) red caviar, real or mock
(optional)**
**125 g (4 oz) fresh seas bass, sea
bream or tuna**
**5 mL (1 tsp) rice or cider vinegar**
**15 mL (1 tbls) green horseradish
powder (*wasabi*), mixed with
cold water to a thick paste**

*Rice patties topped with raw fish*

● ● ● ● ● ● ● ● ● ● ● ● ● ● ● ● ● ● ● ● ● ● ● ● ● ● ●

■ TO SERVE
**sliced tomato, cut radishes,
cucumber strips, onion tassels
and capers (optional)
Japanese soy sauce**

● To make the patties, thoroughly wash the rice in several changes of water until it runs clear, then drain in a sieve for 1 hour.

● Put the rice into a heavy saucepan with a tightly fitting lid. Bury the kelp in the rice. Add 500 mL (2 cups) water, cover and bring to the boil over a high heat. Remove the kelp just before the water boils.

● Reduce the heat to moderate and cook for 5-6 minutes, then reduce the heat to very low and cook for 15 minutes.

● Raise the heat to high for 10 seconds then remove the pan from heat. Let the rice stand for 10 minutes.

● Combine the vinegar, sugar, salt and monosodium glutamate in a small saucepan over moderate heat and heat through. Turn the rice out into a large shallow dish, preferably wooden. Little by little, pour the vinegar mixture over the rice, mixing it with a wooden spatula or a fork, and fanning it vigorously at the same time. Fanning cools the rice quickly and makes it glisten.

● When the rice is cool, wet your hands with water to which a little rice vinegar has been added, and form the rice into about 24 oblong patties, 2.5 cm x 5 cm (1 x 2 in).

● To prepare the topping, bring a small pan of boiling salted water to the boil. Add the vinegar and simmer the shrimps for 1 minute. Drain immediately.

● When cool enough to handle, peel and drain them. Cut the underside from end to end three-quarters of the way through. Then turn them over and flatten them.

● Slice the scallop corals into 2 horizontally. Slice the discs into 3 horizontally.

● Slice the raw fish diagonally into slices 5 mm (1/4 in) thick.

● Spread a dab of *wasabi* paste down the centre of each piece of fish and lay it, horseradish-side down, on top of some patties. Spread the salmon roes directly on some patties and put a dab of paste on top of the roes. Arrange the shrimps on more patties. Arrange the kelp fringe on the side of some patties. Garnish if desired.

● Fill a small bowl with Japanese soy sauce and serve with the patties. To eat, use chopsticks, or fingers, and dip the patties into the soy sauce before eating.

---

*Serve this dish as an appetizer accompanied by a very dry white wine; an Alsacian Tokay for example.*

# ■ SAUTÉED BEEF and VEGETABLES

- *45 minutes*
- *Serves 4*

**500 g (18 oz) sirloin or fillet steak**
**10 green onions**
**1 medium-sized onion, cut into**
**    15 mm (1/2 in) slices**
**240 g (8 oz) tofu, cut into 2.5 cm**
**    (1 in) cubes**
**250 g (9 oz) drained weight**
**    *shiritaki*, or vermicelli**
**500 mL (2 cups) *shungiku***
**    (Japanese chrysanthemum**
**    leaves) or 1 L (4 cups) spinach**
**Chinese cabbage or watercress**
**225 g (8 oz) canned bamboo**
**    shoots, sliced**
**8 button mushrooms, in 6 mm**
**    (1/4 in) slices**
**125 mL (1/2 cup) soy sauce**

**100 mL (3/8 cup) *mirin***
**100 mL (3/8 cup) Japanese stock**
**    (*dashi* — see recipe, p. 16)**
**pinch of monosodium glutamate**
**25 mL ( 1 1/2 tbls) lard or 15 mL**
**    (1 tbls) vegetable oil**
**4 medium-sized eggs (optional)**
**    cooked rice (optional)**

● Freeze the steak for 30 minutes or just long enough to stiffen for easy slicing. Cut in very thin slices, 5 x 4 cm (2 x 1 1/2 in).

● Meanwhile, trim the green onions to include 7.5 cm (3 in) green, then slice into 5 cm (2 in) diagonal slices.

● Cook the shiritaki in boiling water for 1 minute, drain and cut in half, or boil vermicelli for 2 minutes.

*Sautéed beef and vegetables*

● Arrange all the ingredients on a platter.

● In a small saucepan, combine the soy sauce, *mirin*, stock monosodium glutamate and sugar. Bring to the boil, then pour into a small jug.

● When ready to cook at the table, set a cast-iron frying-pan, about 25-30 cm (10-12 in) in diameter, over a table burner and let it heat for several minutes. Rub the pan with the beef suet or swirl round the vegetable oil.

● To cook, add the ingredients to the pan a little at a time; add a little beef and cook 1-2 minutes without turning. Add the spring onions and onion, then pour half of the soy sauce mixture over the pan ingredients. Add half of the noodles, bean curd, green vegetables, bamboo shoots and mushrooms and cook stirring with chopsticks for 3-4 minutes.

● If desired, break the eggs into 4 small individual bowls and stir to blend. Everyone lifts out pieces of the ingredients and dips them into the egg before eating.

● Continue to add the ingredients and cook as above. When finished, cooked rice may be added to the pan. If using an electric frying-pan, start it at 200 °C (400 °F), then reduce it to 130 °C ( 250 °F) when the meat and vegetables are cooked.

# ■ BOILED PORK

* *1 hour 30 minutes*
* *Serves 4*

**700 g (1 1/2 lb) boneless pork loin**
**4 cm (1 1/2 in) pieces of fresh root ginger**
**30 mL (2 tbls) sake**
**60 mL (4 tbls) Japanese soy sauce (*shōyu*)**
**20 mL (4 tsp) sugar**
**1 green onion, white part only, chopped**

● Cut the piece of pork in half so that it fits into a medium-sized saucepan comfortably in one layer. Pour in just enough water barely to cover. Bring to the simmering point, lower the heat and simmer, uncovered, for 1 hour or until the pork is tender. Drain and discard the stock, or put aside for another recipe. Rinse out the saucepan.

● Cool the pork slightly and cut it into 2.5 cm (1 in) cubes. Return the cubes to the saucepan.

● Peel the ginger and slice it thinly. Add it to the pork with the sake, half the soy sauce and 15 mL (1 tbls) of sugar. Add enough water barely to cover. Simmer, covered, over medium heat for 10 minutes.

● Add the rest of the soy sauce and the sugar and simmer, uncovered, until the liquid has evaporated.

● Divide the pork between 4 small bowls. Sprinkle the onion over the pork, and serve.

# ■ SHRIMP OMELETTE

- *15 minutes*
- *Serves 4*

**8 medium-size raw shrimps, shelled and deveined**
**75 mL (1/3 cup) Japanese stock (*dashi* - see recipe, p. 16)**
**4 mL (3/4 tsp) salt**
**2 large eggs, beaten**
**5 mL (1 tsp) sugar**
**15 mL (1 tbls) sake**
**5 mL (1 tsp) arrowroot or cornstarch, mixed with 5ml (1 tsp) water**
**vegetable oil for frying**

● Pound the shrimps to a paste with the back of a heavy knife, or use a blender or food processor.

● Put the shrimps paste into a small saucepan with the dashi and 2.5 mL (1/2 tsp) salt, bring to the boil over medium heat and cook for 1 minute. Cool, drain and set aside.

● In a bowl, combine the eggs, sugar, sake, remaining salt, the mixed arrowroot and the shrimps. Heat an omelette pan or a 20 cm (8 in) frying-pan and add just enough oil to coat the surface.

● Pour the egg mixture and tilt the pan so it covers the whole surface. When the omelette is lightly browned on one side, turn it and brown the other side.

● Slide it out of the pan on to a bamboo mat or a kitchen towel and roll it up.

● When the omelette is cool, remove the bamboo mat or the kitchen towel and cut the omelette into 1.5 cm (1/2 in) slices. Serve as an appetizer.

*Shrimp omelette*

● ● ● ● ● ● ● ● ● ● ● ● ● ● ● ● ● ● ● ● ● ● ● ● ●

# KOREA

With its spicy main dishes and delicious pickled vegetables, Korean cuisine is not as bland as Japanese food and less oily than Chinese. Flavourful and easy to prepare, Korean food is well worth trying.

"A majestic view has no charm if the table is bare," runs an old Korean proverb. Luckily, Korea, nicknamed "the land of morning calm," has both superb scenery and flavourful, attractive food. There are plunging waterfalls, paddy fields, cedar forests, Mongolian desert and wild beaches. The countryside

remains traditional. Its walled villages have reddish-brown roofs of locally made tiles. The men still wear straw hats and baggy trousers tied at the ankle. Many women, young and old, even in the city, wear the traditional *hanpog* – a billowy robe over a full short blouse – so much of the old traditions survive.

Although South Korea is more affluent and has a somewhat warmer climate than North Korea, food in both countries is similar. Seoul, the capital of South Korea, is a high-rise city linked with multiple highways overshadowing walled temples and

*A harbour and city scene in South Korea*

old royal palaces. In its six-storey East Gate Market, 150,000 shoppers a day visit walkways where cooked pigs' heads, squid and fresh chickens are sold beside blankets, quilted cushions and bolts of coloured silk.

With modern methods of production, South Korea today produces more than enough rice for its own needs. Its fishing fleets catch mainly tuna, squid and shellfish, and seaweed also features largely in the people's diet. There is a wide variety of produce such as sweet and white potatoes, radishes, onions, Chinese cabbage, peppers, soya beans and wheat. The local fruit includes apples, pears, persimmons, grapes, peaches, and on the semi-tropical island of Cheju south of the mainland, oranges and tangerines.

Korean cooks are renowned for their artistry in food presentation, but even so their styles of cooking vary from traditional everyday dishes to those from the royal court. The latter include the dish *sinsollo* where meat, eggs, fish, vegetables and nuts are cooked in a tiny brazier and served like a soup.

In South Korean restaurants, a diner orders a main course and the rest arrives automatically. The side dishes include thin transparent noodles with vegetables, rice and 2-3 kinds of pickled vegetables (*kimchi*). A cook's excellence is judge on his *kimchi*: the vegetables must remain crispy and should be served in layers to display their quality. In different parts of Korea the flavourings and ingredients in *kimchi* vary so that at least 30 different types are known.

Politeness, courtesy and hospitality are engrained in Korean life. Flowers, fruit or a cake are taken to a hostess and every guest to a Korean house is always offered a meal. *Bulgogi* (meat strips) and *kalbi* (beef ribs) are the most popular dishes to serve the guests. Food is also associated with the many Korean festivals. Rice cakes and *taro* soup are served for the New Year, and chrysanthemum cakes and wine for the ninth day of the ninth month. Fruit, wine and cakes are taken on a special date to ancestors' graves and, on his first birthday, a child sits amid biscuits, rice cakes and fruit.

Though Western trends are creeping in, South Koreans eat three hearty meals a day. Breakfast includes rice, soup, *kimchi*, clams, seaweed, bean sprouts and fish eggs or octopus with beef. Lunch may be served with noodles instead of rice to make it lighter. Lunch and dinner will be like breakfast with simple or elaborate side dishes depending on the occasion. Vegetables are slightly undercooked, and meat and fish are often cooked over charcoal at the table. Universal seasonings are green onions, sesame seed, sesame oil, garlic, ginger, red and black pepper and soy sauce. Korean food seems hot as red chilies are used in most dishes. Meals end with a soup of boiled rice water with ginger flowers, walnuts, thin slices of pear or lemon zest in it. Fresh fruit is the most common dessert. Hot barley tea in winter or cold barley tea in summer is served with the meal. Wine made from rice, barley and plums, as well as good lagers, are sometimes served.

Ginseng tea is a national passion. The tea tastes slightly musty and is very expensive, but it is said to make one live longer. ∎

# ■ BEEF BALLS

- *30 minutes*
- *Serves 4*

**250 g (8 oz) lean ground beef**
**45 mL (3 tbls) soy sauce**
**1 mL (1/4 tsp) salt**
**pinch of freshly ground black**
**    pepper**
**1 green onion, finely chopped**
**1 garlic clove, finely chopped**
**15 mL (1 tbls) sesame seed**
**30 mL (2 tbls) vegetable oil**
**45 mL (3 tbls) flour**
**2 medium-sized eggs**
**oil for frying**
**vinegar soy sauce to serve**
**    (see recipe, p. 30)**

● Mix the beef in a bowl with the soy sauce, salt, pepper, green onion, chopped garlic, sesame seed and oil. Shape the mixture into flattened rounds, 4 cm (1 1/2 in) in diameter. Roll the patties in flour, then in lightly beaten egg.

● Shallow-fry the patties in a little oil over medium heat until browned on both sides. Serve immediately with vinegar soy sauce for added flavour.

*Serve a lager with this simple dish.*

*Beef balls*

# ■ SEOUL SPINACH SOUP

*This is a favourite soup throughout South Korea. The tender, young spinach leaves transform ordinary beef into a spring delicacy.*

- *1 hour*
- *Serves 6-8*

**250 g (8 oz) chuck or blade beef, thinly sliced and cut into 25 mm (1 in) cubes**
**2 green onions, chopped**
**1 garlic clove, chopped**
**75 mL (5 tbls) soy sauce**
**5 mL (1 tsp) salt**
**pinch of freshly ground black pepper**
**15 mL (1 tbls) sesame seed**
**500 g (1 lb) spinach, washed, trimmed and shredded**

● Put the beef into a large saucepan with the green onion, garlic, soy sauce, salt and pepper and mix well. Cook over medium-high heat for a few minutes until the meat is browned on all sides.

● Add 2 L (9 cups) water and simmer gently for a few minutes, remove any scum, add the sesame seeds and continue cooking 35 minutes or until the meat is tender.

● Just before serving, add the shredded spinach. Simmer until tender, 2-5 minutes.

● ● ● ● ● ● ● ● ● ● ● ● ● ● ● ● ● ● ● ● ● ● ●

# ■ PIQUANT LIVER

*This is a side dish to serve along with kimchi, rice and soup as part of a meal.*

- *About 30 minutes*
- *Serves 4*

**250 g (8 oz) liver**
**30 mL (2 tbls) soy sauce**
**1 garlic clove, chopped**
**pinch of freshly ground black pepper**
**15 mL (1 tbls) sesame seeds**
**5 mL (1 tsp) vegetable oil**
**20-25 mL (4-5 tsp) sugar**
**1 large onion**
**salt**

● Cut the liver into thin slices and then into pieces 4 x 2.5 cm (1 1/2 x 1 in). Put the liver into a small saucepan and add the soy sauce, garlic, pepper, sesame seeds, oil and sugar.

● Quarter the onion and slice each quarter across into 4 slices and add the onion to the liver. Put the saucepan over medium heat and cook for 5 minutes, stirring frequently. Add 150 mL (5/8 cup) water and simmer gently for 10 minutes or until tender. Season to taste with salt and serve.

> *A full-bodied red wine is indicated. Choose among others, a St-Émilion.*

● ● ● ● ● ● ● ● ● ● ● ● ● ● ● ● ● ● ● ● ● ● ●

# ■ GRILLED STEAK FINGERS

*Very popular with visitors to Korea, this beef dish is served over charcoal heaters at table.*

- *Overnight marinating plus 30 minutes*
- *Serves 4-6*

**1 kg (2 lb 3 oz) sirloin steak, cut
across the grain in thin, finger-
sized pieces**
**3 green onions, chopped**
**4 garlic cloves, crushed**
**75 mL (5 tbls) soy sauce**
**30 mL (2 tbls) sesame oil**
**60 mL (1/4 cup) sugar**
**30 mL (2 tbls) medium-dry sherry**
**60 mL (1/4 cup) beef stock
(optional)**
**pinch of freshly ground black
pepper**

● Mix the spring onion and garlic in a bowl and mix in the soy sauce, sesame oil, sugar, sherry, and beef stock if using. Score a cross on each steak finger and mix the steak with the ingredients in the bowl. Leave to marinate for several hours or overnight, covered, in the refrigerator.

● Heat the oven to broil. When it is hot, take the steak fingers directly from the marinade and broil them 5-10 minutes, turning frequently and brushing with the marinade. Serve the meat hot with noodles or rice and *kimchi.*

*Grilled steak fingers*

# ■ COLD PORK and VEGETABLE SALAD

*Here is a really delicious way to enjoy fresh or left-over pork.*

- *1 hour*
- *Serves 4*

**25 g (4 oz) raw or left-over pork**
**5 mL (1 tsp) chopped root ginger**
**5 mL (1 tsp) chopped garlic**
**1 chopped green onion**
**1 medium-sized turnip, peeled and cut into 5 cm (2 in) long, thin strips**
**salt**
**vegetable oil for frying**
**1 small onion, cut into 5 cm (2 in) thin pieces**
**125 mL (1/2 cup) mushrooms, cut into 2.5 cm (1 in) pieces**
**1 small carrot, cut into 5 cm (2 in) strips**
**2-3 celery stalks cut into 5 cm (2 in) pieces or 225-450 g (8 oz-1 lb) spinach, washed and trimmed**
**1 firm, ripe pear**
**30 mL (2 tbls) soy sauce**
**30 mL (2 tbls) sugar**
**pinch of freshly ground black pepper**
**1 L (1/4 tsp) vinegar**
**5 mL (1 tsp) walnut, pine or other nuts, chopped**

● Put the pork in simmering water and cook it until tender, about 25 minutes (or use left-over cooked pork). Allow the meat to cool slightly, then cut it into fine strips 5 cm (2 in) long. Put the strips in a large bowl and add the ginger, garlic and green onion.

● Sprinkle the turnip strips with salt and sauté them in 30-45 mL (2-3 tbls) vegetable oil over medium heat until they are crisp on all sides, 5-7 minutes. Drain on absorbent paper and reserve.

● Simmer the onion and mushroom pieces and the carrot strips in water for 2-3 minutes; drain, refresh under cold running water, drain and reserve.

● Sprinkle the celery pieces, if using, with salt and leave for 10 minutes. Drain the celery pieces on absorbent paper and fry them in 30-45 mL (2-3 tbls) vegetable oil over medium heat for 2-3 minutes or until they become bright green. Drain.

● If using spinach, stir continually in 2-3 lots in 15 mL (1 tbls) vegetable oil in a large frying-pan over medium heat just until tender, 30 seconds to 2 minutes. Add more oil for each lot of spinach.

● Peel, quarter and core the pear. Cut it into thin pieces about 5 cm (2 in) long. Mix the vegetables and pear with the pork. Mix together the soy sauce, sugar, pepper and vinegar and lightly toss this into the pork mixture with 2 forks. Pile the mixture on a serving plate and sprinkle with the chopped nuts before serving.

# ■ KOREAN PICKLED CUCUMBER

*Pickled vegetables or kimchi, is eaten with every meal in Korea. It can be made from many different vegetables but cucumber kimchi is easy to make and crisp in texture. How long the pickle matures depends on the temperature at which it is kept.*

• *30 minutes, plus 2-7 days maturing*
• *Serves 6*

**3 large cucumbers**
**25 mL (1 1/2 tbls) salt**
**1 green onion**
**1/2 garlic clove, finely chopped**
**2 mL (1/2 tsp) finely chopped red chili or a few drops hot pepper sauce**

● Wash the cucumbers but do not peel them. Cut them into 4 cm (1 1/2 in) long pieces. Cut each piece in half lengthways and scoop out the seeds. Sprinkle 15 mL (1 tbls) salt over the cut surface of the cucumbers. Leave to stand for 15 minutes.

● Cut the green onion into 4 cm (1 1/2 in) lengths and slice each piece finely. Wash the salt off the cucumber and put them in an earthware bowl. Add the green onion, garlic, chili and the remaining salt and 150 mL (5/8 cup) water. Mix well and leave to mature. This will take about 2 days in a warm room or about a week in a cold room. Once mature, store in the refrigerator.

# ■ SESAME SOY CHICKEN

*Koreans give their chickens a special savoury treatment by first frying them in sesame oil, then simmering them in a chicken stock and soy sauce.*

- *40 minutes*
- *Serves 4-6*

**1.5 kg (3 1/2 lb) chicken, cut into
  serving pieces
cornstarch for coating
90 mL (6 tbls) sesame oil
60 mL (1/4 cup) soy sauce
60 mL (1/4 cup) chicken stock or
  water
1 large garlic clove, chopped
4 green onions, halved and split
  lengthways**

● Coat the chicken pieces in cornstarch and shake off the excess. Heat the sesame oil in a heavy frying-pan over medium-high heat and fry the chicken pieces until they are crisp on all sides.

● Add the soy sauce, stock or water, garlic and green onions to the pan and cover. Reduce the heat and simmer slowly for 20 minutes or until the chicken is tender, adding more stock or water, if necessary, to prevent the meat from sticking to the pan. Serve with boiled rice and pickled cucumbers (see recipe, p. 29).

For Korean fried chicken, marinate the pieces in the sesame oil, soy sauce, chopped garlic and green onions, finely chopped, for 4 hours, turning the pieces ocasionally. Dry them on absorbent paper, coat with cornstarch, shake off the excess and deep-fry them in hot oil for 5-10 minutes or until each piece is cooked through.

● ● ● ● ● ● ● ● ● ● ● ● ● ● ● ● ● ● ● ● ● ● ● ● ●

# ■ VINEGAR SOY SAUCE

*Beef balls and other fried food are dipped into this simple savoury sauce just before eating.*

- *2 minutes*
- *Makes about 225 mL (1 cup)*

**90 mL (6 tbls) soy sauce
90 mL (6 tbls) vinegar**

**30 mL (2 tbls) sugar
15 mL (1 tbls) walnuts, pine or other
  nuts, finely chopped**

● Mix the soy sauce, vinegar, and sugar together well. Put 30 mL (2 tbls) of sauce in individual dishes and sprinkle with the finely chopped nuts to serve.

● ● ● ● ● ● ● ● ● ● ● ● ● ● ● ● ● ● ● ● ● ● ● ●

# THAILAND

Distinctive and delightfully presented, the cooking of this beautiful Southeast Asian country is charactarized by contrasting flavours – sweet and sour, salty and hot – that meet in a variety of dishes in unexpected ways.

Thai cuisine is not easy to define. Many of the dishes use the Chinese stir-fry technique while an Indian influence can be seen in the curries. But Thai food is not a combination of bits and pieces from the kitchens of the two great countries that lie roughly to its west and east. It is unique in its flavour and its presentation.

Rice is central to any Thai meal. It is a special long-grain rice of exquisite quality and when cooked the grains have a translucent gleam. Thai fruit and vegetables are also splendid and play a large part in the national cookery. And, though not all the fruits and vegetables of Thailand are available in other parts of the world, it is possible to cook authentic Thai food with very little trouble by using a few of the more distinctive ingredients.

The ingredients that dominate the flavour of Thai food is *nam pla* which is made from the filtered liquid produced by fermenting fish with salt. In the West it is sold in Chinese shops as fish soy or fish gravy. *Nuoc nam* is a good substitute.

Another dominant flavour is coriander, of which leaves, stems, roots and dried seeds are all used. The root is especially pungent and, since fresh coriander is nearly always sold with the roots on, it is possible to duplicate the real Thai flavour. Coriander seed is commonly sold on the

*Shellfish in a Bangkok restaurant*

are widely available at Chinese supermarkets. If using them for fried noodle dishes, there is no substitute. Dried shrimps are available cleaned whole, or without heads and tails, at Oriental stores. Other popular ingredients are soy sauce and coconut milk.

*Taramind* pulp is also needed. It is sold in sticky blocks in Indian shops. If the pulp is very dry, a piece of it must be soaked in warm water for about 10 minutes before measuring it.

## Serving a Thai meal

The pattern of a Thai meal is very different from that of a Western meal. Traditionally each diner is presented with a tray on which are a series of china dishes, some covered, some not, and a larger, covered bowl of rice. The meal may consist of rice and about five other dishes including chicken or beef curry, fish, vegetables, salad and dessert and usually a hot sauce.

For cutlery the people of Thailand have adopted the spoon and the fork. Knives are not necessary since meats and poultry are cut into small pieces.

Presentation is important to the Thai cook. Pickled ginger root, which turns an attractive pink in the pickling process, is carved into intricate shapes that take advantage of the root's natural shape.

For a sweet dish, young green coconuts are cut from coconut palms, the top lopped off, the liquid inside poured out, and the creamy flesh scooped from the shell. Then the hard outer husk or shell is pared away, the softer inner shell is sculpted into a an intricate pattern and the top is similarly carved. The cook makes a custard called *sankhaya* which is poured into the shell and baked in a water bath. ■

spice shelves of supermarkets.

The Thai like their food peppery but use chilies more than ground black peppercorns. Using a chili less hot than a Thai cook does not take away authentic flavour from the dish. How hot is a matter of taste.

Garlic, ginger, root, shallots, basil and green onions are also important ingredients. *Laos* or *galingale* is a commonly used spice in the East. It is usually chopped up or ground and sold at specialty food shops. There is no substitute, but omitting it won't ruin a dish. Ground lemon grass, also known as *sereh* powder, is available at many Indian shops and specialty food stores. It has a strong taste and smells of lemon and should be used sparingly. Use grated lemon zest as a substitute. Other popular ingredients are soy sauce and coconut milk.

Chinese rice flour noodles, also known as Chinese rice vermicelli (*py mei fun*),

# ■ SPICY SHRIMP SOUP

- *30 minutes*
- *Serves 6*

**1.5 L (6 1/2 cups) light chicken stock**
**5 mL (1 tsp) ground lemon grass or**
**2.5 mL (1 in) square piece of lemon zest**
**30 mL (2 tbls) lemon juice**
**75 mL (1/3 cup) *nam pla***
**1-2 fresh hot chilies, seeded and sliced or a few drops hot pepper**

■ SAUCE (OPTIONAL)
**45 mL (3 tbls) coarsely chopped coriander leaves**

**6 green onions, trimmed and sliced across thinly**
**250 g (9 oz) frozen cooked shrimps, defrosted**

● Combine the chicken stock, lemon grass or zest, lemon juice, *nam pla* and chilies in a saucepan. Bring to the boil, cover and simmer over low heat for 15 minutes.

● Strain the mixture through a fine sieve into another saucepan. Discard the solids.

● Add the coriander leaves, green onions and shrimps to the stock and simmer over low heat for 2 minutes or until the shrimps are heated through. Serve immediately.

*Spicy shrimp soup*

# ■ FRIED NOODLE SALAD

*This is an extremely popular luncheon dish in Thailand. It can be accompanied by curry or a fish or shellfish dish, or it may be served as the main course with soup and dessert.*

- *1 hour*
- *Serves 6*

**225 g (8 oz) Chinese rice flour noodles**
**15 mL (1 tbls) sugar**
**15 mL (1 tbls) soy sauce**
**15 mL (1 tbls) distilled or white wine vinegar**
**vegetable oil for deep frying**
**3 shallots, finely chopped or small onion, chopped**
**4 garlic cloves, finely chopped**
**250 g (9 oz) boneless pork loin or 250 g (9 oz) boneless raw chicken breast, cut into thin strips**

**250 g (9 oz) flaked crabmeat or shelled shrimps, cut into 1.5 cm (1/2 in) pieces**
**30 mL (2 tbls) *nam pla***
**30 mL (2 tbls) lemon juice**
**4-egg omelette, cut into strips**
**6 fresh red or green chilies, slit in 4-5 places from tip almost to stem end to make "flowers," or 1 small mild red pepper + a few drops hot pepper sauce**
**6 green onions, cut into 5 cm (2 in) pieces**
**coriander sprigs**
**500 mL (2 cups) bean sprouts**

*Fried noodle salad*

● ● ● ● ● ● ● ● ● ● ● ● ● ● ● ● ● ● ● ● ● ● ● ●

● Cover the noodles with hot water and let them stand for 1 minute. Drain and let them dry. Mix together the sugar, soy sauce and vinegar and reserve.

● Heat about 5 cm (2 in) vegetable oil in a wok or deep-fat frier to 220 °C (425 °F) or until a cube of bread will brown in 30 seconds. Fry the noodles, a handful at a time, until they are golden, turning once. Lift them out and drain on absorbent paper. The noodles will break up.

● Heat 60 mL (1/4 cup) vegetable oil in a wok or in frying-pan over medium heat. When hot, stir-fry the shallots or onion and garlic for 30 seconds. Add the pork or chicken breast and stir-fry for 1 minute. Add the crabmeat or shrimps and stir-fry for 1 minute longer. Add the *nam pla* and lemon juice, hot pepper sauce if using, stir to mix and cook for 1 minute.

● Toss the noodles into the meat mixture and pour over the reserved vinegar mixture. Cook over moderate heat just long enough to heat through.

● Turn the noodle mixture on to a large warmed platter and garnish it with the omelette strips, chili "flowers," spring onions, coriander springs and bean sprouts. Serve immediately.

If you can buy uncooked shrimps for this dish, they give the best flavour. However, frozen crabmeat or shrimps can be used instead.

# ■ THAI CHICKEN and MUSHROOM SOUP

*This is a popular soup in Thailand and none of the ingredients are hard to find. It is less hot than Spicy Shrimp Soup, which can be quite fiery.*

* *15 minutes*
* *Serves 4*

**1 garlic clove, crushed**
**15 mL (1 tbls) finely chopped coriander leaves and stalks**
**1 mL (1/4 tsp) freshly ground black pepper**
**15 mL (1 tbls) melted lard, chicken fat, or oil**
**1 L (4 1/2 cups) chicken stock**
**300 mL (1 1/4 cup) mushrooms, thinly sliced**
**30 mL (2 tbls) *nam pla* or anchovy essence**
**125 g (4 oz) boneless cooked chicken breast, cut into thin strips**
**2 green onions, trimmed and sliced across thinly**
**salt**

● Combine the garlic, coriander and pepper in a mortar and pound them to a paste. In a small frying-pan over medium heat, heat the lard, chicken fat or vegetable oil and when hot sauté the garlic mixture for 1 minute. Remove the mixture from the heat and reserve.
● Combine the stock, mushrooms, *nam pla* and the garlic mixture in a saucepan and simmer for 5 minutes. Add the chicken and simmer just long enough to heat it through. Sprinkle with the spring onions, taste for seasoning and add a little salt if necessary.

# ■ BANGKOK STUFFED CRABS

*Small live crabs are used for this dish. The crabmeat is removed from the shells, which are later stuffed with the crabmeat mixture. If small crabs are not available use fresh crabmeat and stuff scallop shells with the mixture. Serve as an appetizer or part of a Thai meal.*

- *1 hour*
- *Serves 6*

**6 small live crabs, or 500 g (1 lb) fresh crabmeat, flaked, and 6 deep scallop shells**
**15 mL (1 tbls) *nam pla***

**5 finely chopped garlic cloves**
**5 mL (1 tsp) finely chopped coriander leaves and stems**
**1 mL (1/4 tsp) freshly ground black pepper**
**75 mL (1/3 cup) coconut milk**
**2 egg whites, stiffly beaten**

*Bangkok stuffed crabs*

**1 egg yolk, beaten with 5 mL
(1 tsp) water
vegetable oil for deep frying
fresh coriander leaves or parsley to
garnish**

● If live crabs are available, drop them into briskly boiling salted water and simmer for about 15 minutes, or until the shells turn bright red.

● Drain the crabs, break off the claws and top shells and remove the meat, flaking it with a fork. Discard any cartilage and gills. Rinse out and carefully dry the shells; set them side. If using crabmeat, have 6 scallop shells ready for the stuffing.

● In a bowl combine the flaked crabmeat with the *nam pla*, garlic, coriander and ground pepper. Stir in the coconut milk, then fold the egg whites into the mixture and pile it into the shells. Brush the stuffing with the egg yolk mixture.

● Put 5 cm (2 in) vegetable oil in a wok or large frying-pan and heat it to 180 °C (340 °F) or until a cube of bread will brown in 45 seconds.

● Fry the stuffed shells in the oil, in 2 batches if necessary, for 3-4 minutes, spooning the oil over the stuffing, until it is puffed and lightly browned. Garnish the shells with coriander leaves or parsley and serve.

# ■ THAI-STYLE FRIED FISH

*Any firm-fleshed, non-oily white fish can be used successfully for this simple dish with its subtle interplay of flavours.*

- *45 minutes*
- *Serves 4*

**90 mL (6 tbls) vegetable oil
1 kg (2 1/4 lb) whole, white-
fleshed fish such as cod,
bass or red snapper
6 green onions, trimmed and cut
into 1.5 cm (1/2 in) pieces
2 garlic cloves, crushed
15 mL (1 tbls) grated fresh ginger
root
45 mL (3 tbls) soy sauce
15 mL (1 tbls) *nam pla*
15 mL (1 tbls) light brown sugar
15 mL (1 tbls) tamarind pulp
1 onion, finely chopped
30 mL (2 tbls) fresh coriander
leaves**

● Heat 60 mL (4 tbls) of the oil in a frying-pan over medium heat and fry the fish until it is brown on both sides, about 5 minutes a side, or until it is done. Transfer the fish to a warmed platter and keep it warm.

● Heat the remaining oil in the frying-pan and sauté the onion, green onions, garlic and ginger for 2-3 minutes over medium heat. Stir in the soy sauce, *nam pla*, sugar and tamarind pulp and cook for 1 minute longer. Garnish with the coriander leaves and serve. Pour the sauce over the fish.

# ■ COCONUT CUSTARD

*In Thailand the husks of small green coconuts are carved to make the baking dishes for this popular dessert. Small ramekins or custard cups, though less picturesque, can be used instead.*

- *1 hour*
- *Serves 6*

**250 mL (9 fl oz) coconut milk**
**250 mL (1 cup) light brown sugar,**
   **slightly packed**
**3 large eggs, lightly beaten**

● In a saucepan over medium heat, combine the coconut milk and the sugar and cook, stirring, until the sugar has dissolved. Remove from the heat and cool for 5-10 minutes.

● Beat the eggs into the coconut milk mixture, mixing thoroughly. Strain it through a fine sieve into six 125 mL (1/2 cup) ramekins or custard cups. Cover each with aluminium foil.

● Set the ramekins in a container that has a cover and pour in enough hot water to come half-way up the sides of the cups. Put the container over medium-low heat to steam the custards for about 30 minutes, or until they are slightly puffed and set. Serve them at room temperature or chilled.

● ● ● ● ● ● ● ● ● ● ● ● ● ● ● ● ● ● ● ● ● ● ● ● ● ●

# ■ THAI CHICKEN CURRY

- *2 hours*
- *Serves 6*

**1.5 kg (3 1/4 lb) chicken, cut into**
   **small pieces, or boned and cut**
   **into 2.5 x 1.5 cm (1 x 1/2 in)**
   **strips**
**400 mL (1 3/4 cup) coconut milk**
**30 mL (2 tbls) *nam pla***
**45 mL (3 tbls) red curry paste**
   **(see recipe, p. 40)**
**1 or more fresh hot green chilies,**
   **seeded and sliced, or several**
   **drops hot pepper sauce**
   **(optional)**
**250 mL (1 cup) basil leaves,**
   **coarsely chopped, or 10 mL**
   **(2 tsp) dried basil**

● Combine the chicken with the coconut milk and *nam pla* in a heavy saucepan and simmer partially covered until the chicken is tender, about 15 minutes, according to the size of the chicken strips.

● Stir in the curry paste and, if you like a very hot curry, add the hot green chilies or hot pepper sauce. Simmer, uncovered, for 5 minutes longer.

Add the basil leaves, stir to mix and serve with boiled rice.

> *A dry white wine (Montagny, Graves) will provide a refreshing contrast to the strong flavour of this dish.*

● ● ● ● ● ● ● ● ● ● ● ● ● ● ● ● ● ● ● ● ● ● ● ● ●

# ■ MANGO SALAD

- *10 minutes plus 30 minutes marinating, then 15 minutes*
- *Serves 6*
- *2 large, slightly under-ripe mangoes weighing about 400 g (14 oz) each*

**15 mL (1 tbls) salt**
**30 mL (2 tbls) vegetable oil**
**50 g (2 oz) loin of pork, coarsely chopped**
**15 mL (1 tbls) finely ground dried shrimps**
**15 mL (1 tbls) coarsely ground peanuts**
**15 mL (1 tbls) *nam pla***
**15 mL (1 tbls) light brown sugar**
**2-3 finely chopped garlic cloves**
**15 mL (1 tbls) finely chopped green onions**

● Peel the mangoes and cut the flesh into large thin strips. Sprinkle them with salt, mixing thoroughly. Let the mangoes stand for 30 minutes.

● Heat 15 mL (1 tbls) of the vegetable oil in a frying-pan and sauté the pork until it is browned on all sides, about 8 minutes. Stir in the ground shrimps, ground peanuts, *nam pla* and brown sugar, cook for about 1 minute and set aside.

● In the remaining oil, sauté the chopped garlic for about 30 seconds until it is lightly browned. Do not let it burn. Transfer it to a small dish. In the oil remaining in the frying-pan sauté the green onions until they are tender. Lift them out of the frying-pan and combine them with the garlic.

● Rinse the strips in cold water and drain. Pat them dry with absorbent paper. Toss the pork mixture with the mango strips, put on a serving dish and sprinkle with the garlic-onion mixture.

*Mango salad*

●●●●●●●●●●●●●●●●●●●●●●●●●●

# ■ RED CURRY PASTE

*This paste will keep one month in the fridge in an airtight container. It is used to flavour poultry and beef or to spice up a mayonnaise.*

• *30 minutes*

**175 g (6 oz) paste**
**30 mL (2 tbls) hot pepper flakes**
**15 g (1/2 oz) dried shrimps**
**3 shallots, chopped, or 1 onion, chopped**
**3 cm (1 1/4 in) ginger, grated**
**4 garlic cloves, chopped**
**5 mL (1 tsp) black peppercorns**
**5 mL (1 tsp) ground coriander**
**5 mL (1 tsp) ground cumin**
**15 mL (1 tbls) fresh coriander leaves, chopped**
**5 mL (1 tsp) ground *laos***

**5 mL (1 tsp) powdered lemon grass or 15 mL (1 tbls) lemon zest**
**30 mL (2 tbls) lemon juice**

● Put the pepper flakes and shrimps in a bowl, cover with hot water and soak for 20 minutes.

• • • • • • • • • • • • • • • • • • • • • • • •

# ■ HOT PEPPER SAUCE

*Traditionally the hot Thai sauces were eaten only with vegetables, either raw or cooked. Nowadays, used with discretion, a chili sauce is served with any fish, meat or poultry dish as well. It is best freshly made but keeps refrigerated up to a week.*

• *30 minutes soaking, plus 10-15 minutes*
• *Makes about 125 mL (4 fl oz)*

**30 mL (2 tbls) dried shrimps**
**3 garlic cloves, chopped**
**10 mL (2 tsp) brown sugar**

**3 anchovy fillets**
**30 mL (2 tbls) tamarind pulp**
**1-2 seeded and chopped fresh hot red chilis, to taste**
**30 mL (2 tbls) *nam pla***
**30 mL (2 tbls) lemon juice**

● Soak the dried shrimps in warm water to cover until softened, about 30 minutes. Drain and combine them with the other ingredients in a blender or food processor fitted with the steel blade and reduce to a paste.

• • • • • • • • • • • • • • • • • • • • • • •

# SINGAPORE and MALAYSIA

Malaysia, with its humid, tropical climate and luscious vegetation, has abundant and varied natural ingredients while Singapore is full of bustling markets selling burning-hot spices and strangely-coloured fruits. All these form the basis for a cuisine that is both spicy and delicate.

With its long coastline and luscious tropical climate, there is a wealth of natural produce, from the wonderful seafoods – crabs, lobsters, oysters, giant shrimps, squid and crayfish – to exotic vegetables such as yard-long beans, palm hearts, breadfruits, water-chesnuts, okra, *loofahs*, bamboo shoots; and taro leaves and fruits like pineapples, mangoes, the delicate *rambutan* and *mangosteen*, and the sweet-tasting *durian*, infamous for its pungent smell. Herbs and spices are an essential part of the Malay kitchen, and many of the bland Chinese dishes have been absorbed and adapted to the local taste by "hotting" them up – either with a spicy chili sauce like crab with chili or by serving a piquant dip as a side dish such as shrimp paste relish. Lemon grass, coriander seeds and leaves, cumin, cardamom, green ginger,

*Lower reaches of the Singapore River*

tamarind, cloves, and aniseed are but a few of the spices used in endless combinations to give different flavours to simple dishes.

A strong Chinese influence is seen in *nonya* cooking, deriving its name from the term *nonya* used to address the wives of the well-to-do Chinese merchants. Rich as they were, they still had to please their husbands and so went to work on the native Chinese dishes, elaborating, adapting and borrowing – particularly from Sumatra and other parts of Indonesia. They added spices for extra flavour and used pork, forbidden to the local Moslems. Today, *nonya* cooking is one of the most varied and enticing cuisines in South Asia.

Indian influence is seen in the piquant, spicy gravy dishes similar to the curries of South India, although not so hot, and in the *sambals* which may be served as a side dishes or, a Malaysian adaptation, combined with other ingredients to form a main course as a *sambal sotong*.

The *saté* (or *satay* in Malaysia) is a classic example of the growth of the Malay kitchen. Undoubtedly originating from the trading Arabs' *kebab*, it has developed into a sophisticated dish, meltingly tender because the meat is marinated before cooking. The Malaysians' love of spicy sauces produced the piquant peanut sauce to accompany the *saté*.

Characteristic of Singapore is the mobile kitchen: Every night after sundown hundreds of stalls are set up – formerly along the roadsides, but nowadays in special areas set aside for them. Each "kitchen" tends to specialize in just one or two dishes and their fame spreads far and wide. One man is so famous for his *char teow* (fried rice noodles) that people travel miles nightly to eat at his stall.

Wherever and whatever one eats in Malaysia there is a marvellous enjoyment of the food, a sense of ritual in the serving of a meal and, in private houses, an overwhelming and abundant hospitality. The recipes that follow will give you an idea of just a few of the dishes that you might be offered if you were a guest in a Malaysian household.

## Unusual ingredients

**Balachan** is a pungent shrimp paste used in very small quantities. For most recipes given here, a piece about 1.5 cm (1/2 in) long will be sufficient. It is sometimes crushed with other spices to make a paste which is then sautéed in a little oil, or it can be grilled or fried on its own before being added to a recipe. It is available from most oriental food stores.

**Candlenuts** are tropical nuts so oily that they can be burned like a candle. When fresh and raw they are indigestable but matured and roasted they are often used in cooking. Brasil nuts make a good substitute, but almonds can also be used.

**Ikan bilis** are young anchovies which have been dried and salted; they are available at most Chinese food shops.

**Salam leaf** is a leaf much used in Southeast Asian cooking. It is similar in appearance and aroma to the bay leaf which may be substituted instead.

**Tamarind water** is made by soaking a piece of tamarind in a little water and then squeezing it. A thickish brown water will come out which should be strained. Repeat the process until you have sufficient for the recipe; 30 g (1 oz) tamarind will make about 300 mL (1 1/4 cup) tamarind water, but it can be made thick or thin as required. The thicker it is, the sourer it will taste.

Another basic ingredient is **coconut milk**, often used to give "body" to a sauce without thickening it too much. Unsweetened coconut milk can be found in many supermarkets but mostly in oriental grocery stores. ■

# ■ SHRIMP PASTE and CHILI RELISH

- *15 minutes*
- *Serves 4-6*

**1 slice *balachan* (shrimp paste)**
**6-8 green or red chilies**
**1 shallot, chopped**
**1 garlic clove**
**salt**
**2 mL (1/2 tsp) brown sugar**
**10 mL (2 tsp) lemon juice**

● Heat the oven to broil, then broil the slice of balachan for 3-4 minutes each side.  Reserve.

● Put the chilies in a small saucepan, cover them with water, bring to the boil and boil the chilies for 6-8 minutes. Remove the chilies with a slotted spoon, then seed and chop them.

● Pound together the chilies, shallot, garlic and grilled balachan, or blend in a food processor or blender.  Season the paste with salt, add the sugar and lemon juice and stir thoroughly. This relish should be used within 24 hours of being made as it does not keep very well.

*Shrimps*

# ■ BEEF SATÉ with PEANUT SAUCE

- *15 minutes, 2 hours marinating, then 20 minutes*
- *Serves 4*

**450 g (1 lb) rump steak, 15 mm (1/2 in) thick**
**2 mL (1/2 tsp) chili powder**

*Beef saté with peanut sauce*

44

**juice of 1/2 lemon**
**10 mL (2 tsp) brown sugar**
**5 mL (1 tsp) salt**
**5 mL (1 tsp) ground coriander or**
   **cumin**


■ FOR THE PEANUT SAUCE
**30 mL (2 tbls) vegetable oil**
**125 mL (1/2 cup) raw, shelled**
   **peanuts**
**2 red chilies, seeded and chopped**
   **or 5 mL (1 tsp) chili powder**
**2 green onions, chopped**
**1 garlic clove**
**1 slice *balachan* — 1.5 cm (1/2 in)**
**5 mL (1 tsp) brown sugar**
**juice of 1/2 lime**
**salt**


● Cut the steak into 1.5 cm (1/2 in) cubes and put into a large bowl with the chili powder, lemon juice, brown sugar, salt and ground coriander or cumin. Mix thoroughly and leave to marinate for at least 2 hours.

● Meanwhile, make the sauce. Put 15 mL (1 tbls) oil in a large frying-pan over medium-high heat, add the peanuts and stir-fry for 2-3 minutes. Remove from the pan and drain on absorbent paper.

● Pound the chilies, shallots, garlic and balachan in a mortar and pestle until it is a smooth paste, or blenderize together.

● Grind the peanuts to a fine powder. Put the remaining oil in a frying-pan over medium-high heat, add the chili paste and fry for 1-2 minutes, then add 175 mL (3/4 cup) water. Bring to the boil, add the ground peanuts, brown sugar, lime juice and a pinch of salt, and stir over a medium heat until the sauce is thick, about 10 minutes. Put into a bowl and keep warm.

● Heat the oven to broil.

● Thread the beef cubes onto bamboo skewers, 5 cubes per skewers, and broil for 10 minutes or until the meat is done, turning the skewers several times. Serve with the peanut sauce handed round separately.

---

*A red wine would clash with the peanut sauce. Instead, serve a dry white wine.*

---

## ■ YELLOW RICE in COCONUT MILK

• *1 hour soaking, then 30 minutes*
• *Serves 6*

**350 g (12 oz) long-grain rice**
**30 mL (2 tbls) oil or clarified butter**
**5 mL (1 tsp) ground turmeric**
**600 mL (2 1/2 cups) thick coconut**
   **milk**
**5 mL (1 tsp) salt**
**1 salam leaf or bay leaf**

● Soak the rice in cold water for 1 hour, then rinse and drain it.

● Heat the oil or butter in a saucepan over medium heat, add the rice and sauté it for 1-2 minutes.

● Stir in the turmeric and sauté the rice for a further 1 minute.

● Add the coconut milk, salt and salam leaf and boil over medium heat until the rice has absorbed all the liquid, about 10 minutes. Lower the heat, cover the pan tightly, and cook for a further 10 minutes. Or, if you are worried about the rice sticking, put it into a steamer and steam for 10 minutes.

● When the rice is cooked, discard the salam leaf, pile the rice into a serving dish and serve hot.

## ■ FRIED ANCHOVIES and PEANUTS

• *20-30 minutes*
• *Serves 6 as part of a larger meal*

**225 g (8 oz) dried salted anchovies**
   **(*ikan bilis*)**
**250 mL (1 cup) raw, shelled**
   **peanuts**
**175 mL (3/4 cup) oil**

● Heat the oil in a wok or a large frying-pan over medium-high heat. Add the peanuts and fry for 4-5 minutes, stirring continuously. Remove the peanuts with a slotted spoon, and drain on absorbent paper.
● Break off and discard the heads of the anchovies. Fry them in the remaining oil for about 2 minutes, stirring all the time. Remove from the wok and drain on absorbent paper.
● When the anchovies and peanuts are cool, mix them together in a bowl and serve.

# ■ SQUID in RED CHILI SAUCE

- *30 minutes + 10 minutes cooking*
- *Serves 4-6*

**1 kg (2 1/4 lb) squid**
**15 mL (1 tbls) white wine vinegar**
**5 candlenuts or basil, or**
　　**7 almonds**
**6 large red chilies, seeded and**
　　**chopped, or 30 mL (2 tbls)**
　　**paprika**
**6 shallots or 1 onion**
**1 slice *balachan* (optional)**
**5 mL (1 tsp) ground ginger**
**2 mL (1/2 tsp) ground cumin**
**2 mL (1/2 tsp) turmeric**
**pinch of lemon grass**
**30 mL (2 tbls) oil**
**45 mL (3 tbls) tamarind water**
**5 mL (1 tsp) brown sugar**
**salt**

● Clean the squid, removing the tentacles and discarding the ink sack and the head. Chop the tentacles into 1.5 cm (1/2 in) lengths and remove the bone.  Cut the body into small squares.  Rinse these in 575 mL (6 cups) cold water mixed with 1 mL (1 tbls) vinegar.  Drain the squid and discard the liquid.

● Pound the nuts, chilies (if using), shallots  and balachan into a very smooth paste, or put through a food processor. Mix in the paprika (if using), ginger, cumin, turmeric and lemon grass.

● Heat the oil in a wok or large frying-pan over medium-high heat, add the paste and sauté for 1 minute before adding the squid and tamarind water. Sauté for 3 minutes.

● Add the sugar, salt and 150 mL (5/8 cup) water and continue cooking, stirring freqeuntly, for 5-6 minutes. Transfer to a deep serving bowl and serve immediately.

# ■ STUFFED BRAISED CHICKEN

- *3 hours*
- *Serves 6*

1.8 kg (4 lb) chicken
salt and freshly ground black
    pepper
150 mL (5/8 cup) oil
5 potatoes, peeled and sliced
6 green onions, sliced
2 garlic cloves, crushed
2 red chilies, seeded and very
    thinly sliced, or 5 mL (1 tsp) red
    hot pepper flakes
175 g (6 oz) lean ground beef
pinch of freshly grated nutmeg
2 eggs, beaten

5 tomatoes, blanched, skinned,
    seeded, and chopped
30 mL (2 tbls) soy sauce
275 mL (10 fl oz) light stock

● Bone the chicken except for the wings
and drumsticks. Sprinkle some salt and
pepper over the chicken and leave it in a
cool place while you prepare the stuffing.

● Heat 60 mL (4 tbls) oil in a large
frying-pan over medium-high heat,
add the sliced potatoes and cook for

*Stuffed braised chicken*

10-15 minutes until they are done. Remove from the pan, mash them and leave to cool.

● Heat 45 mL (3 tbls) oil in a wok or frying-pan. Add the shallots, garlic and chilies, or pepper flakes, and fry over medium-high heat about 3 minutes, stirring continuously. Remove the mixture from the pan and let it cool.

● Mix the ground beef and mashed potatoes together, then add the green onion mixture. Season with salt, pepper and freshly grated nutmeg, add the beaten eggs and mix well.

● Put the stuffing into the chicken, pressing well in, and sew up the chicken with a trussing needle and strong thread.

● Heat 60 mL (4 tbls) oil in a large saucepan over a medium heat. Add the chicken and fry over high heat for 8-10 minutes until nicely browned, turning it several times.

● Add the chopped tomatoes and soy sauce, then cover the pan and simmer very slowly for 1 hour 20 minutes, uncovering the pan every 10 minutes and adding 45 mL (3 tbls) stock to the pan. Prick the chicken each time with a fork, and turn it over.

● At the end of this cooking time, the sauce should be rich and thick, so if necessary reduce it by boiling fast for 5 minutes. Then transfer the chicken onto a large, warmed service platter and slice thickly. Taste the sauce, adding salt or soy sauce if necessary and pour over the chicken. Serve immediately with yellow rice in coconut milk and fried bamboo shoots.

# ■ SAUTÉ of BAMBOO SHOOTS

• *30 minutes*
• *Serves 2-4*

**50 g (2 oz) dried shrimps**
**450 g (1 lb) canned bamboo shoots**
**30 mL (2 tbls) oil or butter**
**5 shallots, sliced, or 1 large onion,**
**    chopped**
**2 garlic cloves, sliced**
**2 red chilies, seeded and sliced**
**    or 2-5 mL (1/2-2 tsp) red hot**
**    pepper flakes**
**30 mL (2 tbls) light soy sauce**
**salt**

● Soak the shrimps in cold water for at least 10 minutes, then drain.

● Rinse the bamboo shoots under running cold water and slice them thinly, then cut the slices into small squares.

● Heat the oil or butter in a wok over medium-high heat, add the shallots, garlic and chilies and sauté for 2-3 minutes, stirring continuously. Add the shrimps and soy sauce, stir for a further 1 minute, then add the bamboo shoots, stir-frying for 2-3 minutes longer. Check for seasoning and serve hot.

# ■ SHRIMPS and VERMICELLI SOUP

- *2-2 hours 30 minutes*
- *Serves 4-6*

**125 g (4 oz) pork tenderloin or chicken breast**
**175 g (6 oz) raw shrimps, shelled**
**22.5 mL (1 1/2 tbls) vegetable oil**
**5 shallots, finely sliced or 1 large onion, chopped**
**2 garlic cloves, crushed**
**5 mL (1 tsp) ground ginger**
**5 mL (1 tsp) ground coriander**
**2 mL (1/2 tsp) turmeric**
**175 g (6 oz) rice vermicelli (*laksa*)**
**300 mL (1/4 cup) coconut milk**
**250 mL (8 oz) tofu, cut into thick strips**
**250 mL (1 cup) bean sprouts**
**salt and freshly ground black pepper**
**5 green onions, thinly sliced, to garnish**

● Put 600 mL (2 1/2 cups) water in a saucepan, season with salt and pepper, add the pork or chicken, and boil for 45 minutes. Remove the meat with a slotted spoon and chop into small pieces. Reserve the stock.

● Heat the oil in a wok or a deep saucepan over high heat, add the shallots and sauté for 1 minute. Add the garlic, ginger, coriander and turmeric, stirring for another 30 seconds before adding the shrimps and the meat. Fry for a further 1 minute then add the stock and simmer for 25 minutes.

● Place the vermicelli in a saucepan, pour over the boiling water, cover and leave for 5 minutes. Drain the vermicelli.

● Add the vermicelli and the coconut milk to the wok and continue simmering very gently for 15-20 minutes until the coconut milk starts to boil. Stir well, add the tofu strips and beansprouts and simmer for 5 minutes, stirring from time to time.

● Pour the soup into warmed bowls, garnish with the thinly sliced green onions and serve immediately.

# INDONESIA

Food is precious in Indonesia, even sacred, but it is enjoyed with uninhibited pleasure. Its strong but subtle flavours are influenced by Chinese and Indian cooking, but they are unmistakably different. Dishes such as *saté* – small marinated, boiled meatballs – are world-famous, but these islands also have specialties to tempt even the dullest palate.

Among the 300 inhabited islands of the vast archipelago are the Spice Islands where spices have been traded for many centuries. Most Indonesian dishes call for at least a pinch of three or four of them, or more. In addition, there are the powerful, distinct flavours of onions and garlic, peanuts or soya beans. The beans are usually fermented to make soy sauce or *kecap* from which comes the English word "ketchup." (The letter "c" in modern Indonesian is always pronounced "ch" as in "*church*.") There are also many varieties of chilies, from the mild, green *lombok hijau* to the ferociously hot, fire-red *cabé rawit*.

But Indonesian cooking is not just a matter of spices and strong flavours; the basic ingredients are just as important. Though Java and Bali give a first impression of having a vegetable-based cuisine, meat and fish play major roles in all local cooking. No town is more than half a day's journey from the sea, and seafish and shellfish, including squid and crabs, can be bought almost everywhere. In the past the fish had to be dried and salted before it was taken

*Elaborate temple offerings in Bali*

inland by bullock cart, and salted fish are still very popular. Freshwater fish are caught in the rivers or flooded fields, or farmed in artificials ponds.

Frogs are widely available and are considered a delicacy. Flocks of ducks are everywhere, marching out in the morning and rallying in the late afternoon to begin the journey home.

In Hindu Bali, meat is usually either poultry, lamb or pork. The rest of Indonesia is generally muslim and in Java beef replaces pork. In West Sumatra there are few cows and the most common meat is goat or buffalo. The Minangkabau people, who live in the high hills of West Sumatra, eat plenty of meat to keep out the cold. In their favourite dish, *rendang*, meat is cooked for several hours in spices and coconut milk until it becomes quite dry and almost black. The meat will then keep, even in a tropical climate, for several weeks.

Most Indonesians regard a meal as essentially a one-course affair. The rice and savoury dishes are all put on the table together and the diners help themselves as they please, starting and finishing more or less when they like. Fresh fruit usually follows this main course at a dinner party. The standard drink all through the meal is Java tea with no milk but with a lot of sugar. Westerners also enjoy lager or full-bodied red wine during the meal.

## Unusual ingredients

**Santen**, also known as coconut milk, is made by soaking desiccated unsweetened coconut in warm water for 2-3 minutes, squeezing the coconut between your fingers, then straining the mixture through muslin, pressing the coconut well to extract all the liquid. Alternatively the coconut and water are mixed in a blender for 15 seconds, then strained in the same way. Use 250 mL (1 cup) coconut for 60 mL (1/4 cup) water.

The desiccated coconut is discarded. This then produces coconut milk. *Santen* can also be made by dissolving creamed coconut, sold in a block like lard, in hot water; for each 25 g (1 oz) of creamed coconut, add 75 mL (1/3 cup) water. This method yields thick coconut milk. Refrigerate *santen* and use within 24 hours of making. Use *santen* made with desiccated coconut when making slow-cooked dishes. Add *santen* made with creamed coconut only at the end of cooking to thicken sauces.

**Laos** or **galingale** is a commonly used spice in the East. It is a tuber that looks like an iris root or ginger root. *Laos* is usually chopped up or ground.

**Lemon grass** is a typical grass, but has a bulbous base and a strong taste and smell of lemon. It is sold dried in most Indian shops. It is used like bay leaves in a dish, and removed before the dish is served. Powdered lemon grass is also available but should be used sparingly as its taste is much more concentrated.

**Tauco** are fermented and salted yellow or black soya beans. Sold whole in cans, they are mashed to a smooth paste and used to make savoury, aromatic sauces. The beans can be stored in a covered jar in the refrigerator for up to 4 months.

**Tahu** or **bean curd** is made from fermented soya beans. It is sold by Chinese supermarkets in the form of a soft, white cake. It can also be bought in jars. Store tahu in cold water in the refrigerator for up to 2 days. Do not freeze it.

**Soy sauce** is sold either "dark" (sweet) or "light" (clear and salty) in Chinese shops.

**Tamarind** water adds sourness to dishes. Cut or break off a 25 g (1 oz) chunk from a block of tamarind and soak it in 275 ml (10 fl oz) warm water. Press and squeeze the piece of tamarind so the water takes up the sour flavour and brown colour. Strain the water before using. ■

# ■ CHICKEN with SALTED YELLOW BEANS

*Tauco are soya beans that have been partially fermented and then salted. You can buy black or yellow salted beans in cans at Oriental food stores. The yellow salted beans are used in this dish because they make a more attractive sauce.*

- *1 hour*
- *Serves 4*

**1.6 kg (3 1/2 lb) chicken, cut into serving pieces**
**2 onions, sliced**
**4 garlic cloves, crushed to a paste**
**30 mL (2 tbls) vegetable oil**
**15 mL (1 tbls) salted yellow beans, crushed to a paste**
**10 mL (2 tsp) dark soy sauce**
**5 mL (1 tsp) brown sugar**
**2 mL (1/2 tsp) chili powder**
**5 mL (1 tsp) paprika (optional)**
**5 mL (1 tsp) ground ginger**
**125 mL (1/2 cup) tamarind water**

● Fry the onions and garlic in oil in a large saucepan or flameproof casserole fo 30 seconds. Add the yellow bean paste, stir, then add the chicken pieces. Stir the chicken so that every part is coated with the soya bean mixture.

● Add the soy sauce, 250 mL (1 cup) water and all the remaining ingredients; cover and simmer over low heat for 45 minutes. Remove the lid and continue cooking for 5 minutes to reduce the sauce. Serve the dish hot, with boiled rice.

*Chicken with salted yellow beans*

## ■ MINCED PORK SATÉ

*This recipe comes from Bali, though there are variations of it on nearby islands. On Lombok, for example, they make it with beef. The minced meatballs may split when you push them on the bamboo skewers unless you take the precautions described below. You can prepare this saté and refrigerate it for up to 24 hours before cooking.*

* *30 minutes*
* *Serves 4*

**500 g (1 lb) boned leg or tender loin of pork with a little fat, minced**
**3 garlic cloves, minced**
**1 red chili, crushed, or 2 mL (1/2 tsp) red hot pepper flakes**
**2 mL (1/2 tsp) powdered ginger**
**5 mL (1 tsp) coriander seeds, lightly roasted and crushed**

**5 mL (1 tsp) brown sugar**
**10 mL (2 tsp) soy sauce**
**15 mL (1 tbls) tamarind water**
**30 mL (2 tbls) grated fresh or desiccated coconut**
**1 egg, beaten**
**salt**

■ FOR THE SANTEN
**250 mL (1 cup) desiccated, unsweetened coconut or 25 g (1 oz) creamed, unsweetened, grated coconut**

*Minced pork saté*

● First make the santen. If you are using desiccated coconut, soak it in 60 mL (4 tbls) hot water for 3 minutes, squeezing the coconut between your fingers. Strain the liquid through muslin to extract all the liquid and discard the coconut. If you are using grated creamed coconut, add 90 mL (6 tbls) hot water and stir to dissolve it.

● Mix the crushed garlic and chili with the ginger, coriander, sugar, soy sauce and tamarind water. Stir 2 mL (1/2 tsp) of this mixture into the santen. Keep the rest of the mixture in a cool place until the saté is ready to grill.

● When ready to grill, mix the remaining spice mixture with the meat and add the desiccated coconut, the egg and salt to taste. Shape the meat into small balls about he size of walnuts. Do not thread the balls on the skewers until the last possible moment.

● Heat the grill to medium. At the last moment, thread the meatballs on to the bamboo or metal skewers and place them under the grill. Cook for 4-5 minutes, turning them from time to time, until the meat is firm. Take the satés from the grill and brush them lightly with the spiced santen. Continue grilling and turning the meat until the balls are golden brown. Single balls of this *saté*, served on wooden cocktail sticks, are delicious as appetizers to serve before a meal or with drinks.

---

*Serve with an equally spicy wine. A Spanish Rioja would be a good choice.*

---

# ■ INDONESIAN FRIED SQUID

*This is a popular dish in many areas and cannot be said to belong to any one island, though it is more often found near the coast than island.*

- *20 minutes, plus at least 2 hours marinating*
- *Serves 4*

**700 g (1 1/2 lb) squid**
**60 mL (4 tbls) tamarind water**
**2 mL (1/2 tsp) turmeric**
**5 mL (1 tsp) powdered ginger**
**pinch of chili powder**
**4 shallots, sliced or 1 onion, chopped**
**3 garlic cloves, crushed**
**2 mL (1/2 tsp) salt**
**5 mL (1 tsp) dark soy sauce (optional)**
**vegetable oil for frying**

● To clean the squid, cut off the head and tentacles, peel off the violet "skin," throw away the head and the ink sack, pull out the backbone and wash the flesh under running cold water.
● Slice the body into thin rings and cut the tentacles into lengths of about 25 mm (1 in). Mix the tamarind water with all the other ingredients except the oil and leave the squid in this liquid to marinate for 2 hours or more.
● Drain the squid, dry on absorbent paper and discard the marinade. In a large pan heat the oil to 180 °C (350 °F) or until a bread cube browns in 60 seconds. Fry the squid for 5-6 minutes and serve hot with rice.

# ■ CRISPY-FRIED CHICKEN with SAVOURY RICE

Nasi *is the Indonesian word for cooked rice.* Nasi kebuli *is almost a meal in itself and needs no more than the addition of vegetables or a green salad.*

- *1 hour soaking, plus 1 hour 30 minutes*
- *Serves 4*

**1 1/2 kg (3 1/2 lb) chicken, cut into several pieces**
**500 mL (2 cups) long-grain rice**
**3 garlic cloves, crushed**
**4 shallots, crushed, or 1 onion finely chopped**
**10 mL (2 tsp) ground coriander**
**2 mL (1/2 tsp) cumin**
**pinch of ground *laos***
**pinch of powdered lemon grass or a stalk of fresh lemon grass**
**1 small cinnamon stick or 5 mL (1 tsp) ground cinnamon**
**pinch of grated nutmeg**
**2 whole cloves**
**salt**
**vegetable oil for deep frying**

■ FOR THE GARNISH
**1 small onion, sliced in rings, fried in oil and drained on absorbent paper**
**chopped parsley**
**chopped chives**
**sliced cucumber**

● Soak the rice in cold water for 1 hour. Mix the crushed garlic and shallots with the spices and salt to taste. Put the chicken pieces and the spice mixture into a saucepan and fill the pan with cold water until the chicken is just covered. Place the saucepan over high heat and when the liquid boils, reduce the heat and simmer the chicken until it is tender, about 40 minutes.

● Meanwhile, wash the rice several times in cold water and drain it well. Sauté the rice for 5 minutes in a large saucepan with 15 mL (1 tbls) of the oil, stirring it continuously. Strain the stock from the cooked chicken and make it up to 500 mL (2 cups) with water if necessary. Add this to the rice, then boil the rice in the stock until all the liquid has disappeared, about 10 minutes.

● While the rice is cooking, heat the oil in a deep-fat frier to 180 °C (350 °F) or until a cube of bread will brown in 60 seconds. Dry the chicken on absorbent paper then deep-fry them for 8-10 minutes or until the outside is crisp.

● Serve the rice piled up in the middle of a large warmed serving dish, arrange the chicken around the outside of the rice and sprinkle over the onion rings, parsley, chives and cucumber slices.

For a tasty alternative to chicken, use pork loin cut in 2.5 cm (1 in) cubes.

# ■ SPICY MEAT SOUP

- *1 hour 30 minutes*
- *Serves 4*

**500 g (1 lb) beef brisket**
**125 g (4 oz) raw or cooked shrimps, peeled**
**6 shallots or 2 onions, chopped**
**3 garlic cloves**
**30 mL (2 tbls) oil**
**2 mL (1/2 tsp) ground ginger**
**pinch of chili powder**
**2 mL (1/2 tsp) turmeric**
**salt**
**10 mL (2 tsp) lemon juice**

### ■ FOR THE GARNISH
**1 onion, sliced in rings, fried in a little oil and drained on absorbent paper**
**flat-leaved parsley, chopped**
**lemon wedges**

● Cover the brisket with salted water and boil for 1 hour, skimming the surface from time to time to remove any scum. Meanwhile, chop and finely mince together the shrimps, shallots and garlic.

● Drain the meat, allow to cool slightly, and cut into bite-sized cubes, reserving the stock. Sauté the shrimp mixture for 1 minute in the vegetable oil. Add the ginger, chili powder, turmeric, salt and 250 mL (1 cup) of the stock, cover and simmer for 7-8 minutes.

● Put the meat cubes in another saucepan, strain over the shrimp mixture and discard the solids left in the strainer. Simmer the meat for 2 minutes before adding the rest of the stock. Bring the soup to the boil and simmer for a further 20 minutes.

● Add the lemon juice and serve the soup hot, garnished with the fried onion rings, flat-leaved parsley and lemon wedges in heated bowls.

*Spicy meat soup*

# ■ INDONESIAN STUFFED MARROW or ZUCCHINI

This recipe is from Sulawasi, the large island that used to be known as Celebes. It is made there with a petola, a young loofah (squash) that has not yet developed the fibrous inner skeleton which is sold as a bath sponge or flesh brush. A small marrow or large courgette (zucchini) is an excellent substitute.

- 1 hour 30 minutes, plus cooling
- Serves 4-6

**2 small vegetable marrows or large zucchinis**

■ FOR THE STUFFING
**4 eggs**
**salt and freshly ground black pepper**
**vegetable oil for greasing**
**15 mL (1 tbls) vegetable oil**
**5 shallots or 1 small onion, thinly sliced**
**2 green chilies, seeded and sliced into thin rounds, or 2 mL (1/2 tsp) chili powder**
**250 g (8 oz) minced beef or chicken breast, minced**
**125 g (4 oz) peeled shrimps, chopped**

● Heat the oven to 180 °C (350 °F). If marrows are used, peel them thinly. Cut the marrows or zucchinis down the middle lengthways, scoop out the seeds with a spoon or melon baller and discard them. Cover the marrow or the zucchini halves with cold, salted water.

● To make the stuffing: reserve the white of one egg and beat the yolk with the rest of the eggs. Season with salt and pepper. Grease a 20 cm (8 in) frying-pan with a little vegetable oil, then heat the pan. Pour enough of the beaten eggs in to make a thin omelette and cook over medium heat for 3-4 minutes.

● Turn on to a plate to cool. Repeat until all the beaten eggs are used, greasing the pan with vegetable oil before cooking each omelette, and leaving the cooked omelettes to cool while you prepare the rest of the stuffing.

● Sauté the shallots or onions and chilies or chili powder in 15 mL (1 tbls) vegetable oil over low heat until they are soft. Mix the meat with the shrimps, add them to the shallots and chilies and stir over medium heat for 3-4 minutes, then add the reserved egg white and mix well.

● Remove the marrow or zucchini halves from the water and dry them with absorbent paper. Roll up the omelettes, cut them into thin slices and mix them gently into the meat mixture. Fill two of the marrow or zucchini halves with the mixture and cover with the other marrow or zucchini halves. Place the stuffed vegetables on a baking sheet and bake in the oven for 40-50 minutes. Serve cold, cut into thick slices.

The marrows or zucchini can be steamed rather than baked for 40-50 minutes.

# ■ PANCAKES with COCONUT FILLING

- *2 hours for the batter to stand, plus 45 minutes*
- *Makes 14-16 pancakes*

**300 mL (1 1/4 cup) flour**
**4 mL (3/4 tsp) salt**
**3 eggs**
**45 mL (3 tbls) melted butter or vegetable oil**
**250 mL (1 cup) milk**
**clarified butter or vegetable oil for greasing**

■ FOR THE FILLING
**75 mL (1/3 cup) brown sugar**
**400 mL (1 5/8 cup) desiccated, flaked coconut or fresh young coconut, grated**
**1 cinnamon stick or 5 mL (1 tsp) ground cinnamon**
**pinch of salt**
**5 mL (1 tsp) lemon juice**

● Sift the flour and salt into a bowl. Beat the eggs and stir them into the flour with the melted butter or oil. Stir gently until smooth. Gradually add the milk. Strain the batter through a fine sieve and dilute with a little water, if necessary, to give the batter the consistency of thin cream. Leave the batter to stand for 2 hours.
● Make the filling. Bring 250 mL (1 cup) water to the boil in a saucepan, add the sugar and stir until it is dissolved. Then add the coconut, cinnamon stick and salt. Simmer the mixture gently over low heat until the coconut has absorbed all the water. Put in the lemon juice, stir for 1 minute, then discard the cinnamon stick. Keep the filling warm while making the pancakes.

● To make the pancakes, heat a 12-18 cm (5-7 in) pan and grease it with a little clarified butter or vegetable oil. Spoon in just enough of the pancake batter to thinly coat the bottom of the pan, turning the pan to distribute the batter evenly.
● Cook the pancake for 1 minute over low heat and carefully turn it over using a flexible spatula or palette knife. Cook the pancake for 1 minute on the other side.
● Repeat until all the pancake batter is used, greasing the pan before cooking each pancake. When they are ready, fill each one with 15 mL (1 tbls) of the filling, roll them up and serve immediately.

# ■ SPICED BEEF in COCONUT

• *3 hours 30 minutes to 4 hours*
• *Serves 6*

**1 1/2 kg (3 1/2 lb) beef brisket or good stewing steak, cut into 4 cm (1 1/2 in) cubes**
**6 shallots, crushed or 2 onions, chopped**
**3 garlic cloves, crushed**
**5 mL (1 tsp) ground ginger**
**5 mL (1 tsp) turmeric**
**15 mL (1 tbls) chili powder**
**2 mL (1/2 tsp) powdered *laos***
**salt**
**1 bay leaf**

**■ FOR THE SANTEN**
**1.5 L (6 cups) – 500 g (1 lb) desiccated, unsweetened coconut**
**1.7 L (7 1/2 cups) hot water**

● First make the *santen*. Soak the desiccated coconut in the hot water for 3 minutes, squeezing the coconut between your fingers. Strain the mixture through a muslin inside a sieve, squeezing the coconut to extract the liquid. Discard the coconut.

● Mix the crushed shallots and garlic, the ginger, turmeric, chili powder, *laos* and a little salt with the *santen* in a wok or frying-pan. Add the meat and bay leaf and and let the mixture simmer gently over low heat, stirring from time to time, until the liquid becomes thick, 1 1/2-2 hours. Taste and add more salt if desired.

● Continue cooking the mixture over a low heat, stirring from time to time, until all the sauce has been absorbed into the meat, 1 1/2 - 2 hours. Then stir the meat continuously in the remaining oil, until it is golden brown all over, about 30 minutes. Do not overcook or the chunks of meat will flake and desintegrate.

● Serve the meat hot with plain boiled rice. If you have stored it, reheat it at 180 °C (350 °F) or in a pan over low heat.

# RECIPES INDEX

61

# ■ Vol. 4: CHINA

# ■ Vol. 5: VIETNAM • JAPAN • THAILAND • KOREA • MALAYSIA • INDONESIA

Minced pork saté, 54
Omelette stuffed with spinach, 15
Pancakes with coconut filling, 59
Piquant liver, 26
Red curry paste, 40
Rice patties topped with raw fish, 18
Sauté of bamboo shoots, 49
Sautéed beef and vegetables, 20
Seoul spinach soup, 26
Sesame soy chicken, 30
Shrimp omelette, 22
Shrimp paste and chili relish, 43
Shrimps and vermicelli soup, 50
Spiced beef in coconut, 60
Spicy meat soup, 57
Spicy shrimp soup, 33
Squid in red chili sauce, 47
Stuffed braised chicken, 48
Thai chicken and mushroom soup, 35
Thai chicken curry, 38
Thai-style fried fish, 37
Vegetable salad, 8
Vinegar soy sauce, 30
Yellow rice in coconut milk, 46

## ■ Vol. 6: SPAIN • PORTUGAL • GREECE • EGYPT • MOROCCO

Almond biscuits, 16
Almond fingers, 60
Andalusian Gazpacho, 5
Baked eggs, gypsy-style, 10
Catalan fish stew, 20
Chicken tajine, 58
Chili and nut sauce, 19
Couscous Royale, 54
Cucumber and yoghurt salad, 46
Curly endive salad with cold meat, 16
Dried fruit salad, 49
Egg and lemon soup, 38
Eggplant salad, 35
Fried squid rings, 11
Garlic shrimps, 17
Garlic soup, 15
Grilled spring chicken, 47
Lamb and pepper stew, 18
Lamb baked in packets, 42
Lentils with rice, 48
Lisbon-style liver, 29
Madrid stew, 22
Meat and okra stew, 48
Mixed chopped salad, 45
Moroccan layered chicken pie, 56
Moroccan spicy meat balls in sauce, 57

Moussaka, 36
Mushrooms à la grecque, 38
Orange, date and walnut salad, 53
Paella valenciana, 8
Palace bread, 50
Piquant casseroled chicken, 25
Pork with mussels, 27
Portuguese green cabbage soup, 26
Portuguese onion purée, 31
Portuguese-style fried cod, 30
Salt cod and vegetable omelette, 28
Sardine relish, 26
Sea bass with orange sauce, 7
Siphnos cheese and honey pie, 41
Spicy shrimps, 59
Steamed walnut pudding, 32
Stuffed tomatoes, 46
Sweet Easter bread, 40
Taramosalata, 39
Valencia chocolate mousse, 12
Wrinkled potatoes with red sauce, 6

## ■ Vol. 7: LOUISIANA • CALIFORNIA • MEXICO • SOUTH AMERICA

Avocado and olive omelette, 18
Avocado aspic, 17
Avocado dip, 15
Bananas Foster, 12
Beef stew in olives, 21
Berry grunt, 32
Boston baked beans, 28
Boston brown bread, 29
Broad bean salad, 49
Café brûlot, 9
California date-nut bread, 22
California stuffed loaf, 20
Californian fish stew, 16
Chicken pie with corn topping, 50
Chicken stew Bogota-style, 58
Chocolate rum punch, 60
Columbian avocado sauce, 5
Colombian cheese dessert, 60
Colombian potatoes with cheese sauce, 57
Corn oysters, 30
Corn relish, 26
Corn soup, 53
Cranberry mould, 26
Deep-fried yeast cakes, 5
Duckling with rice, 48
Fish chowder, 25
Frisco crab, 19
Garlic olives in oil, 18
Guacamole, 39

## ■ Vol. 8:
## SOUTH OF FRANCE

© MARSHALL CAVENDISH 1992.
© TRANSCRIPT PUBLISHING, 395, boul. Lebeau, Saint-Laurent (Québec)  H4N 1S2.
Division of Transcontinental Publications Inc. Member of Groupe Transcontinental G.T.C. Ltd.

• General manager: Pierre-Louis Labelle• Marketing manager: Robert Ferland • Administrative assistant: Dominique Denis • Editor in chief: Danielle Champagne • Reviser: Martine Gaudreault • Proofreaders: Services d'édition Guy Connolly • Creative Director: Fabienne Léveillé • Computer graphics designers: Lan Lephan, Badin-Côté Design

Legal Deposit: 4ᵗʰ quarter 1992 - Bibliothèque nationale du Québec - Bibliothèque nationale du Canada